What Others Are Saying About
David and Lisa Frisbie's Previous Books

■ ■ ■ ■

Happily Remarried

"Upbeat yet realistic…a gold mine of practical information in a user-friendly format."

—ArmChairInterviews.com

"Commonsense and biblically grounded approach…I only wished that I had the book 20 years ago when after a painful divorce, I eventually found the courage to remarry…I will [recommend] it to anybody who brings up the subject of remarriage."

—**Dave Garcia,** Bookstore Manager, North Coast Church, Vista, California

"The four key strategies for marital unity are superb and practical."

—**Paul and Pauline Hicks,** retired pastors

"I read this book three times the week I bought it. It's already helped me with my husband's kids…My husband stayed up late one night and read the whole book. It's great for anyone trying to raise a stepfamily. I highly recommend it."

—**Jaimie Fisher,** reader

■ ■ ■ ■

Moving Forward After Divorce

"The Frisbies write with a poignancy and practicality that acknowledges the hard realities but points to hope rather than resignation."

—**Ed Robinson, PhD,** President, MidAmerica Nazarene University

"David and Lisa Frisbie know how to get the broken unstuck from their place of anguish. The book is laid out in a plain and simple way with answers that have been tested time and again."

—**Chuck Millhuff,** Revivalism Coordinator, The Church of the Nazarene, Olathe, Kansas

"An effective way to offer people healing and hope following the painful experience of divorce…Scores of relevant illustrations and very practical, biblically based insights reinforce the guidelines the Frisbies suggest."

—**Dr. Dan Casey,** Senior Pastor, First Church of the Nazarene, Little Rock, Arkansas

Raising
Great Kids
On Your
Own

DAVID & LISA FRISBIE

HARVEST HOUSE PUBLISHERS
EUGENE, OREGON

All Scripture quotations are taken from the Good News Translation—Second Edition © 1992 by American Bible Society. Used by permission.

Cover by Koechel Peterson and Associates, Minneapolis, Minnesota

Cover photos © iStockphoto; photos.com

Statement About Privacy and Identification

Persons and couples appear in this book in one of two ways:

Where persons or couples are mentioned using *both* first and last names, these persons or couples are either public figures, or have consented in writing that we may tell their stories, identifying them and/or quoting them by name. We are grateful to those who have not only told us their stories, but have also allowed us to identify them.

Where persons or couples are mentioned using first names only, certain key details of the story (including but not limited to names, location, marital status, number and gender of children) have been altered to prevent identification of the subjects while retaining the integrity and nature of the narrative. We have found that single parents, perhaps even more so than other adults, highly value their privacy and their anonymity.

With regard to first-name-only stories, any resemblance to any person of the same name, or in the same location, or in a similar situation, is therefore entirely coincidental.

RAISING GREAT KIDS ON YOUR OWN
Copyright © 2007 by David and Lisa Frisbie
Published by Harvest House Publishers
Eugene, Oregon 97402
www.harvesthousepublishers.com

Library of Congress Cataloging-in-Publication Data
Frisbie, David, 1955-
  Raising great kids on your own / David and Lisa Frisbie
    p. cm.
  ISBN 978-0-7369-1941-8 (pbk.)
  1. Single parents—religious life. 2. Parenting—Religious aspects—Christianity.
I. Frisbie, Lisa, 1956- II. Title.
  BV4596.S48C53 2005
  248.8'45—dc22

                                                            2006030638

Printed in the United States of America

    09 10 11 12 13 14 15 / BP-SK / 12 11 10 9 8 7 6 5 4 3 2

■ ■ ■ ■

To some of the wise and wonderful people who teach us,
not only by their words,
but also by their consistent faith-filled lives

■ ■ ■ ■

Acknowledgments

■ ■ ■ ■

Among the wise and wonderful people to whom this book is dedicated are Stephen and Kathie Smith, two of the best parents we've met along our journey. While raising Jeff, Ginger, Brittany, and Tori (four of our favorite people!), Stephen and Kathie have demonstrated the love, patience, understanding, and endurance that great parents learn and practice. We are always learning from these helpful, generous friends.

Steve and Marj Miller provided us with a "retreat" in the form of a cabin in Montana's Beartooth Mountains near Yellowstone Park. Is there a better place to write and reflect, to pray and talk with God? Joining us for mountain hiking, they also brought along Kelsey, Aaron, and Annie—blessing our journey with the insights of children. Steve and Marj are godly parents and good friends.

Bob and Crissa Evanoff have modeled compassion and Christian service for us. While raising Samuel and Claire, they have blessed us greatly with practical support and much-needed encouragement. Bob is a greatly gifted composer, arranger, multi-instrument musician, and worship leader. He is also a designer, inventor, and successful businessman. Crissa is a radiant and godly teacher, mentor, and guide, who enjoys raising the two young lives in her own household. Bob and Crissa have ministered to us when we needed ministry the most: Both of them exemplify Christ's love in action.

Finally, we offer our deep thanks to those who instruct us in the faith. Among these are Larry Osborne, Chris Brown, Charlie Bradshaw, Paul Savona, Gary Vanderford, and other pastoral staff. Our debt to these leaders cannot be repaid during our earthly lifetimes. We are challenged, stretched, admonished, and encouraged as these leaders speak the truth of God's Word into our lives. From their messages and from their examples, we are always learning.

Contents

■ ■ ■ ■

What If Your Children Have a Bright Future? 9

PART ONE

Finding Your Way to a New You—
Learning to Care for Yourself

1. Adventures in Faith 19
2. Building Your Support Network 31
3. The Role of Community in Raising Your Children 45
4. Taking Care of Yourself 57

PART TWO

Helping Your Kids Adjust to Trauma and Change—
Learning to Nurture Your Children

5. Appropriate Grieving 77
6. Telling Your Story 91
7. Raising Children Means Learning 109
8. How to Communicate with Your
   Older Children and Teens 125

PART THREE

Facing the Future—
Learning to Manage Your New Life

9. Working In and Working Out:
   Employment Issues for Single Parents 147
10. Completing or Continuing Your Education 161
11. Money Matters: Financial Reality and
    Your Life as a Single Parent 177
12. Dating and Relationships 191

Living It Out: Learning from One
Single Parent's Experience 205

Where Would You Like to Go Today? 219

Resources for Single Parents 225

Thanks to Our Partners in Writing 233

What If Your Children Have a Bright Future?

■ ■ ■ ■

As we write this book, the current Most Valuable Player in the National Football League is a young running back named Shaun Alexander. He's set new records for rushing yardage, touchdowns made, and several other categories. He is arguably—at least for this season—the best-known name in the NFL.

Those who know Shaun best—those who watched him play football for Alabama and participate in the Fellowship of Christian Athletes, Youth for Christ, and other activities—insist he is much more than a fine athlete. He is also an outstanding person: a man of character, strong values, and a sense that serving others matters more than promoting yourself.

Shaun Alexander is a success in life, and he is one other thing too: He is the son of a single parent.

Baseball star Rickey Henderson was only a few months old when his father abandoned the family. Rickey's mother moved to Pine Bluff, Arkansas, with her eight children. Aided by a support network that included her parents (Rickey's grandparents), this courageous woman worked hard to provide for the financial needs and personal well-being of her kids.

Later, when Rickey was being offered a choice between football scholarships and playing baseball, it was his mother who suggested that he "stick to baseball." Rickey did, becoming a star with the Oakland Athletics and the New York Yankees.

Actress Lauren Bacall is known for her many accomplishments in films, her nominations for Oscar awards, and her loving marriage to Humphrey Bogart. Respected and admired across decades and even generations, Bacall is one of Hollywood's most famous success stories. She also was raised by a single parent.

Ed Bradley, reporter for CBS News, is probably best known for his work on the popular program *60 Minutes*. Ed's parents separated soon after he was born, and he grew up living with his mother during the school year. Ed was essentially raised by his mother, although he spent summers (while out of school) at his father's home. Ed became a substantial and respected journalist and television personality, known across the country and around the world.

Alexander Haig, former White House Chief of Staff and Secretary of State, lost his father when he was only ten years old. Alexander took a variety of jobs to help support the family while his mother worked hard to make ends meet. Raised by a widowed single mom, Al Haig grew up to travel the globe, negotiate complex agreements and treaties, and serve several presidents with distinction and honor.

■ ■ ■ ■

So what does the future look like for *your* children?

Do you feel like their future is limited, their options are few, and that there are serious limits to what they can accomplish? The examples of Rickey Henderson, Lauren Bacall, Alexander Haig, and now Shaun Alexander (among many others) suggest otherwise.

Life is more than being successful, and fame can be fleeting. Yet the point is this—instead of seeing yourself as an "unfortunate" single parent who is doomed to raise "limited" or "disadvantaged" children, take a look at the stories behind the achievers in today's headlines. Behind many of these successes is a single parent doing her or his best in the midst of hardship, suffering, and loss. These difficulties did not prevent dedicated single mothers and fathers from raising accomplished, successful kids.

In his book *The Seven Habits of Healthy Families,* Stephen Covey tells the story of a young woman who found herself divorced at age 19, left to raise a 2-year-old son by herself. Without a high-school degree, her future looked bleak.

Fast-forward. At the end of Covey's story is a confident woman who speaks to large groups, telling her experience and encouraging others. She helps to develop a scholarship program for low-income women. She has not only finished her high-school education, she has also attended community college, gone on to receive a four-year degree, and then attended graduate school and earned an MBA.

She has raised children who themselves are well-educated, and who are using their education to serve others. The woman's son—born when she was just 17 years old—has a job helping people with disabilities. He is working on his master's degree. The woman's daughter, who is completing her college studies, serves as a volunteer teaching English as a second language.

Looking back at her life, this woman sees a transition from being someone in great need herself (a divorced single mom, 19 years old, raising a 2-year-old son) to being a person who helps those in need—an example being followed by the rest of her family.

The point is clear. This woman didn't merely "survive" as a single parent—she went on to achieve greatness in the parts of life that really matter. She raised great kids, and she taught them—by her own example—to help others.

Now it's your turn.

PART ONE

Finding Your Way to a New You—Learning to Care for Yourself

When Jared left her, Bryanna's entire world fell apart.

Within days of walking away, her husband mailed her a thick folder of legal papers, announcing that he was filing for a divorce. Bryanna hardly had time to think or react—she was mostly in shock.

In the days and weeks after being abandoned, she soon quit eating, quit spending money, and rarely left her small apartment. Alone for the first time since leaving for college, she spent restless nights tossing and turning, imagining the worst. In the first month that her husband was gone she lost 11 pounds and experienced a near-constant cough and sore throat.

She was the mother of two young children, now the only parent on duty. Josiah was three at the time—Amber was barely ten months old. Raising the kids by herself seemed impossible, especially without the income from Jared's sales job at a popular electronics store. Between his regular salary and his frequent bonuses, Bryanna hadn't needed to work during their five-year marriage.

Friends phoned, but Bryanna couldn't find the strength to answer her phone or return their calls. Neighbors offered to help but seemed unsure of what she might need or want. Her mother, a divorced woman who lived in another state, was cynical and unsympathetic.

"All men are alike," Bryanna remembers her mother saying soon after Jared left. "You might as well learn that now, while you're still young."

Not yet 30, Bryanna didn't feel young. She felt old, incompetent, and totally incapable of raising her two young children. She had no idea where to begin looking for work. If she did find work, who would watch the kids?

The sheer hopelessness of her situation weighed on her day and night. "I thought about killing myself," she admits today. "I thought about it a lot. Sometimes I dreamed about it at night. Then I'd look at Amber and think *She needs me,* and that would keep me from hurting myself."

But even loving her young son and daughter was not always enough. "I remember thinking that maybe my kids would be better off without me, better off if somebody else raised them," Bryanna sighs. "I spent days thinking like that, days when I felt like I was the worst mom in the whole world. I didn't want to get out of bed, didn't want to face my kids. I didn't want to do anything."

Today her life is different, yet Bryanna remembers clearly how hopeless and alone she felt in the months after Jared left her. "It was the worst time of my life—the absolute worst. I hated Jared, I hated my mom, and most of all I hated myself."

Desperate for anything that might help, Bryanna tried smoking marijuana, a habit she had dabbled in briefly in high school but since abandoned. The drug gave her a temporary sense of relief but soon became an overall negative.

"I'd feel calmer while I was smoking pot," she recalls. "Then a half hour later I'd feel guilty about how much money I'd spent. I would end up feeling worse after smoking than I felt before. It just wasn't worth it."

With her emotions spiraling downward out of control, Bryanna found help where she may have least expected it. In the pages ahead, we'll talk about the source of her lifeline; we'll also look at helpful resources that other single parents, both women and men, have found at the times of their deepest suffering.

■ ■ ■ ■

Before we do, let's look at the underlying reason why it's important for single moms and dads to reach out for help. Simply stated, if a single mother doesn't learn how to function effectively alone, she may not be able to care for her children. If a single father tries to drown his sorrows in alcohol or lives for months with untreated depression, his ability to care for his children will suffer.

Before a single mother can learn how to successfully care for her children, she often needs to learn healthy ways to care for herself. It's a lesson we find ourselves teaching over and over as single parents burn out on feelings of depression, anger, and loss. Left untreated, these normal emotions deplete the parent's emotional and physical resources, which means that sooner or later—usually sooner—the children will suffer in many ways.

As we begin our extended look at self-care for struggling single parents, let's imagine we're about to take a flight to a nearby city. We roll our luggage down the ramp, find our seats, and wait for the plane to depart.

When the boarding door finally closes, flight attendants move down the aisle. One of them grabs a microphone and begins the speech that precedes every airline flight originating in the United States.

"In the event of a sudden loss of cabin pressure, oxygen masks will appear in front of you. Place the mask over your nose and mouth and pull down on the tube to begin the flow of air to the mask. Oxygen will be flowing to the mask even if the bag does not fully inflate."

Then comes the part of the announcement that nearly every mom or dad is likely to ignore in the rush of an in-flight emergency:

"If you are traveling with a small child or someone in need of assistance, secure the mask over your own face before assisting other passengers."

Why does the FAA require this announcement? What is the logic behind this endlessly repeated watchword of air travel?

The answer is simple: A mom who is distracted by her screaming child, flailing around trying to secure a mask over her young son's face, is likely to forget that she herself needs to breathe. She will become so absorbed in the challenges at hand—the struggle to help her child survive—that she'll forget to place the mask over her own face. As her supply of oxygen dwindles, the busy parent will lose consciousness…and will no longer be able to care for the child she loves so dearly.

The child will be at risk, and may even perish, because a frantic mother forgot to take care of her own health during a moment of crisis and emergency.

Becoming a single parent is usually a moment of crisis and emergency. Whether it occurs after the death of a partner or whether it follows a divorce or unplanned pregnancy, becoming a single parent challenges our emotional and mental health. It is a crisis of hope and confidence for most of us.

While it is normal and natural for a single parent to fixate on the needs of her or his children, it is absolutely essential for parents without partners to learn healthy habits of self-care and appropriate self-nurture. In the chapters of this section we'll look at four sources of strength that can point a single parent in the direction of balance and composure amid life's daily problems.

If you feel alone and stressed as a single parent, one or more of these sources of strength may be a positive direction for you to choose.

Adventures in Faith

When Your Journey Raises
More Questions Than Answers

■ ■ ■ ■

*When we finally come to the end of our
own security, we begin to learn the
meaning of faith and spirit.*

EVELYN ROYCE

Bryanna was rescued by a girlfriend.

Even though it sounds too simple, the reality is, a caring girlfriend refused to go away when Bryanna didn't return her calls or respond to her e-mails. Instead, the friend kept calling, kept sending e-mails. Eventually she came over and rang the doorbell, and stood and waited outside the door of Bryanna's apartment.

Bryanna opened the door.

It was a visit that changed her life, though not all at once. In fact, at the time, Bryanna remembers she was mostly upset that her friend wouldn't respect her need for privacy.

"I almost didn't open the door," she admits. "I thought about pretending I wasn't home—but where else would I be?"

Bryanna opened the door, and her friend came to her rescue.

Carrie, her friend, brought a simple message. "You need to get out of the house," Carrie told her. "Quit sitting around here all the time. You end up thinking too much!"

Bryanna remembers her response clearly. "I told her that I couldn't afford to go anywhere. But she wouldn't take 'no' for an answer. Instead, she started telling me about all the free things we could do. She just wouldn't shut up."

Bryanna declined Carrie that day, but her friend kept calling and dropping by for visits. One day, she invited Bryanna to a movie night at a nearby church. The church, a start-up in the growing neighborhood, held its services and events at a middle-school gymnasium. The movie night was free and included free child care.

■ ■ ■ ■ ■

"It was just so peaceful in there…Nobody was preaching at me, this wasn't even a 'church' night."

■ ■ ■ ■ ■

"How could I pass that up?" Bryanna asks rhetorically. "It was a free movie for me, plus free child care for my two kids. I actually considered dropping the kids off at the church, then going somewhere else. But at the last minute I decided I'd better stay in the gym, in case Josiah or Amber had a problem."

Bryanna's son had fun in the church-provided child-care area. Her daughter slept in a portable crib during the whole event. Bryanna, munching on fresh cookies while drinking several cups of complimentary decaf, remembers feeling calmer and more at ease than she'd felt since Jared left her.

"It was just so peaceful in there," she remembers. "Nobody was preaching at me, this wasn't even a 'church' night. It was just sponsored by the church group. I think somebody might have said a prayer before the movie, but I honestly don't even remember that for sure.

"The whole thing was relaxing. I think I really did sleep during part or all of the movie. It was the first time I felt like I could just let go…"

Driving home from the movie with her two kids asleep in the back of Carrie's car, Bryanna decided that getting out of the house had been a good idea. When Carrie asked about future events, she replied that she would try the church again, maybe even for a regular worship service.

■ ■ ■ ■

A few days later she received an e-mail message from a church pastor. "I had signed some kind of attendance sheet during movie night," she tells us. "I wasn't too worried about it because I was already getting tons of mail from nearby churches anyway. I didn't put down my phone number; I didn't want anyone bothering me or trying to call. But it seemed okay to give them my e-mail address, so I did. I can always delete messages."

The pastor's e-mail to Bryanna that day was a short announcement about the next three movie nights, held once each month on a regular schedule. The note also contained a link to the church's Web site.

Bryanna clicked on the link for a quick look. "I learned a whole lot of things by doing that. Probably the most important thing I found out was that they were starting a new Saturday-night praise service. It sounded a lot like the movie night: Child care was provided free, plus the cookies and coffee were free."

Despite her reservations about "getting religious" she made her way to a praise service a few Saturdays later. She remembers being highly conflicted about going to the event, not certain she was doing the right thing.

"If there was a God—and I didn't really believe in that at the time—then I was mad at Him," Bryanna confesses. "How could God let me get married to a guy who was going to leave me and the kids? How could God let me suffer so much pain from being rejected and left all alone? So even though I was going to a church event, it wasn't because I was buying into all that God-stuff."

Bryanna's experience at the movie night had lowered her anxiety level about attending church. It had felt great to spend nearly two hours around young, energetic people who seemed happy with their lives and relaxed around each other.

"It really drew me in," she tells us. "It was contagious. I'd had a rotten day before going to that first movie night, but once I got there, everyone was friendly and low-key. I didn't realize how much

I'd missed just being around other people, just having normal social interaction with people close to my own age."

The Saturday praise event felt much the same. Although she didn't know the words to the songs, Bryanna was drawn to the dynamic energy at work in the school gym: pulsing music driven by guitars and drums—some people sitting, some standing, others even dancing. It was a very different experience from her distant memories of going to church during her childhood.

"That first Saturday I went, somehow being there in the gym with all that music and so much positive energy—it just really helped me," Bryanna says.

It was Bryanna's first visit to this kind of church experience, but it wouldn't be her last. Drawn by the music, the cookies, and also by the free care for her children, she began making the Saturday-night praise gathering a regular part of her weekly schedule. She found herself looking forward to it after a week spent coping with depression, lethargy, and loss.

■ ■ ■ ■

One Saturday night Carrie suggested that Bryanna might want to talk with one of the female counselors among the church staff. She was closed to the idea at first, but began to think about it in the next few weeks.

"I finally decided that it couldn't hurt, and it might even help," she admits. "I decided that if it didn't cost me anything, I would go ahead and try it."

Bryanna began seeing a female counselor from the church, with the first three visits being free because of Bryanna's money situation. After the first three visits, the counselor explained, there would be a small charge if Bryanna chose to continue with the sessions. The church had several scholarships available if even the small cost seemed insurmountable.

The sessions went surprisingly well, and she chose to continue. Once a week she began venting her anger, her pain, and her unresolved questions in the office of a caring, compassionate counselor. "I just let it all out. After one visit, I realized that I didn't need to hold anything in, I just could let it fly. So I did."

In the midst of all that venting and when she least expected it, Bryanna also found God. Or perhaps it was the other way around.

"I think God found me," she says in talking about her religious experience. "I think God was waiting for me to start paying attention again. I'd gone to church when I was a kid—I'd even made a 'decision for Christ' at a camp once when I was little. But I got a long way away from that when I went off to college. And church had never been part of my life as an adult."

■ ■ ■ ■

After the praise service one Saturday evening, Bryanna found herself walking to a corner of the gym where church members were available to pray with anyone wanting some prayer. Although Bryanna intended merely to ask for prayer for her difficult life as a single parent and for issues surrounding her increasingly messy divorce, instead she found herself asking questions about God. She asked about prayer and whether it really worked.

"I was talking to this older woman," Bryanna says. "She didn't seem threatened at all by my lack of belief, or whatever. She just listened. When I was done she told me I could receive God into my life right then and there, if I wanted to do it. She wasn't pushy about it; she wasn't trying to get me to say a bunch of words or make some kind of commitment.

"It was more like—'God is right here in this building, would you like to experience Him for yourself?' And even though I wasn't sure I believed any more, something inside me said 'yes' and I prayed with her to receive God into my life."

It sounds simple, we comment.

"It was," she reflects. "I had been going to the counselor and expressing my feelings, but this was different. I was talking to this woman about prayer and about God, and she was kind of like—why not right now?"

Bryanna explains that her religious experience is now personal and real, and that it has continued to affect the rest of her life.

"There are a lot of days when my life totally sucks," she says with disarming candor. "But even on those days, I don't feel alone anymore. I can tell that God is with me; He gives me the strength I need to keep moving forward."

■ ■ ■ ■

Bryanna reconnected with the faith of her childhood, returning to church attendance after an absence of more than a decade. In doing so, she connected not only with faith but also with tangible resources: counseling, pastoral staff, music, new friends and peers. In addition, she enjoys the sheer relief from parenting that a few hours of weekly child care provides for her.

Her transition from doubt to faith began with a free movie.

We ask Bryanna to explain what her faith means today, if she can.

"I still have a lot of questions," she says slowly. "I'm not sure why my life has worked out this way. Josiah is starting school; I know kids will ask him about his dad. What is he supposed to tell them? I worry about how he'll respond if the kids at school tease him about not having a daddy."

Bryanna talks about both of her children for a while, then returns to the topic of her personal faith and its impact on her life as a single parent. "I think mostly it's about not being alone. I spend so much time feeling alone as a single parent, but finding faith means I'm not really alone while I'm doing this. I feel like God gives me wisdom; I know He gives me strength when I need it, which is pretty much all the time.

"I'm going to a small-group Bible study when I can; it depends on whether I can get somebody to watch the kids," she continues. "I'm learning more about God and about what faith really means. But for me, it's about not being alone anymore. It's about having a partner— God—who's always there for me; He's always there for my kids."

Lighting the Way Home

Michael's return to his childhood faith was an adventure in computer navigation.

As a cash-strapped single dad, he found himself shopping for a reliable used car. He picked up car-trader magazines, devoured classified ads in the daily newspaper, and also checked online ads, always looking for good deals.

When he found the car of his dreams, he found a lot more besides.

"I saw this ad on Craigslist," Michael recounts. "I was looking for a used Honda Accord or Toyota Camry, something reliable but older with a lot of miles on it—so it would be cheap."

His dream car was for sale in Forest Lake, a wooded suburb north of his home in St. Paul, Minnesota. Michael did a search for the address on his computer. Driving out to look at the car in a borrowed vehicle, he recalls how peaceful it seemed to get out of the city. The drive to Forest Lake took him past lakes and trees, beaches, and parks. The farther he got away from the city, the more his tension seemed to melt away.

"The car was for sale on a farm, basically," Michael remembers. "They had washed the car and parked it by the side of the road near their driveway when I came out to see it."

Michael immediately connected with the car's owners, an older couple with teen children. Somehow—he does not remember how—the topic of church came up during the conversation. He discovered that the car's owners were Catholics, both involved in a small-group renewal movement within the broader framework of the church.

Within a few minutes Michael forgot about the car and found himself swapping notes with the couple, comparing church experiences with them.

"Their story was a lot like mine," he says. "I was raised Catholic but quit going to Mass when I was a teen. I just didn't find any meaning in it—it all seemed so routine and mechanical, just going through the motions.

"They said the same things, but they also said they'd really reconnected with God lately. They were meeting with a small group of

"It's like God was lighting my way home."

other people from their parish to study the Bible and to pray for each other."

Michael did buy the car, a decision he explains took all of a few seconds.

"It was in great shape," he tells us. "It had almost 200,000 miles on it, but it looked pretty good for its age. I was ready to buy it when I drove up."

Meanwhile, the drive to Forest Lake produced an unexpected side effect, taking Michael in a new direction he hadn't anticipated.

"We talked for probably three hours that first time I went out there," he says. "The car was almost an afterthought, once we started to really talk and get acquainted. Before I left, they asked if they could pray for me, right then and there. The woman put her arm on my shoulder, and they both prayed for me. While they were praying I just felt this…peace."

The couple invited him to join their Bible-study group when he could. They even offered to find him a babysitter in Forest Lake, so the young father could bring his kids along on Bible-study night.

"It was a package deal," he laughs. "They were taking away all the possible reasons I couldn't come up there and join them for prayer."

■■■■

Eighteen months later, Michael still often makes the drive to Forest Lake to meet with the group. In doing so, he has come to a newfound faith while still embracing the religion of his culture and heritage.

"We're all Catholics," he notes, "and we all plan to remain Catholic. But the thing is—what we have together in our group is something we can't seem to find within the walls of the church. It's a strong sense of God's presence; a real feeling of connecting with God when we pray and study together.

"Somewhere in those first few meetings I just felt God sort of fill me, sort of come into my life in a new way. I'm learning to identify that as God's Spirit, the part of God that connects with us as people and makes us family with Him. I heard about Jesus, Joseph, and Mary, but nobody told me that God could fill us with His Spirit and guide us with His wisdom. Or maybe they did mention it and I just kind of tuned it out."

Has Michael returned to Mass as well?

He nods his head affirmatively.

"It has more meaning for me now," he says quietly. "It's the same thing it always was, but it means more now. I don't go every week; I don't get to Mass as often as I make it to our prayer group. But yes, I am going to Mass again, and yes, I am finding it more meaningful than it was when I was younger."

Michael's return to his childhood faith began with test-driving a used car.

"It's like God was lighting my way home." Michael smiles. "And he used the headlights of an old borrowed car to show me the way."

Faith and the Not-So-Empty Nest

Carla rediscovered her faith when she moved into her former bedroom after Greg divorced her. Alone with two children under age five, Carla didn't have the income to rent even a small apartment in her expensive Southern California locale. She made the only decision that seemed logical to her—she moved back home with her parents.

"Mom and Dad were glad to see me come home, even with kids," Carla says with a bright smile. "They gave me my old room back; they gave the kids my brother's room. Mom and Dad have a split-level, Brady Bunch–type house with four bedrooms, and it was down to just the two of them living there."

Not that everything was ideal by any means.

"It was weird, like I regressed in age to my teens," she admits. She was 29 when she moved back in; her thirtieth birthday party was held in the same dining room where her childhood birthdays had been celebrated.

"My boys drove Mom and Dad crazy at first," she remembers. "They were noisy and active, typical boys, but Mom and Dad hadn't been around that kind of energy level for a while. We all had to adjust to each other."

Carla saw the move as temporary, something to tide her over until she could find a job that would support her family in a nearby apartment or condo. Nearly three years later, Carla is still living in her parents' home.

"It's temporary," Carla says shaking her head. "At least that's what I thought it was going to be. I never dreamed I'd be here three years after Greg left. Sometimes I can't believe I'm in my 30s and still living at home."

The return to faith seemed natural and familiar for Carla.

"We all went to church with Mom and Dad that first Sunday after I moved home," she explains. "It was the obvious thing to do. They have a minivan, and we all piled in and went to church that day.

"Greg and I hadn't been going to church, we'd both been too busy. So it had been ten years or so since I'd attended my home church. What amazed me was how much 'the same' everybody was. It was like nothing had really changed at that church in almost a decade."

The impact on Carla was immediate and life-changing. "I started crying as soon as the choir started to sing. I don't know why, but when they started singing I just sat there crying. My boys looked up at me and you could see in their faces—they wondered why I was so sad all of a sudden."

Carla was not sad; she was deeply moved by the memories of how real God had seemed all those years ago, growing up in her small, family-oriented church. Gifted in music, she had frequently sung in the choir as an older child and then during her teen years. Now as an adult, memories of God's presence in the music flooded her with an overwhelming sense of the reality and nearness of the God she'd been avoiding for a while.

"It was coming home," she says, choking up a little. "On one level I had moved back into my parents' house. But on a deeper level I was coming home to a way of believing, a way of acting, that I had drifted pretty far away from."

■ ■ ■ ■

Carla made an appointment to talk with the pastor's wife. She soon found herself pouring her heart out to a woman she barely knew—the pastor had come to the church during Carla's absence. Still, the two women bonded quickly.

"She told me she herself was a child of divorce," Carla recalls. "She started crying when she told me some things about her childhood. It really helped me feel more at ease, more normal, less like I was something weird."

Gently and graciously, the pastor's wife led Carla to consider reconnecting with the faith of her childhood. It was a step she was ready to take—she claims she didn't feel pushed or pressured to make the choice.

"Not at all," Carla insists. "I knew in my heart it was the right thing. I just needed to hear it from somebody else, somebody outside my own family."

She made a public declaration of her recommitment to God at a Sunday-evening service in the small church. Closely watched by her two boys, she later was baptized during a Sunday-morning worship service, the oldest of four candidates for baptism on that particular morning.

For Carla, the return to faith has helped her cope with a difficult life.

"My ex has cheated me at every possible turn," she says of the divorce settlement and its outcome. "I hired a lawyer, but I couldn't afford to pay very much. My ex got pretty much everything he wanted. I'm responsible for half of our debts during the marriage, even though I wasn't the one spending the money."

Carla estimates that she'll be in debt for at least a decade.

"And that's with living at home," she comments. "Which I'm not sure we can do forever. Mom and Dad have been great, and my boys don't seem to mind, but I'd still like to get a place of our own."

Meanwhile, she senses God's presence in the midst of her difficulties.

"The pastor's wife is probably my closest friend now," Carla confides. "She prays with me, she gives me advice, she really understands what I'm dealing with. It helps so much that she grew up with a single mom after her own father walked out on the family. Maybe that's why we relate to each other so well."

■ ■ ■ ■

Carla's story serves as a useful bridge to our next chapter. In addition to exploring the role that faith can play in nourishing and comforting a divorced man or woman, we'll take a look at the support to be found within our own families, and sometimes also in the families and among the relatives of our ex-partners.

For single parents, more so than with most other adults, it's important to realize that in spite of how we feel, we are definitely not alone.

Building Your
Support Network

It May Be as Close
as Your Family Circle

■ ■ ■ ■

*In a strange way, it's almost like the divorce
healed my relationship with my parents and with
my sister. It's like we're a family again.*

JUDITH, SINGLE PARENT, AGE 34

Gary's wife walked out the door and never came back. Eventually, several years later, Gary filed for a divorce. His lawyers had a difficult time locating his ex-partner, who was living in another state and using a completely different first name and last name.

In the end there was the closure and structure of a divorce, but for nearly five long years until the divorce went through Gary lived not only with feelings of rejection and abandonment, but also with complete uncertainty about his future. Was Marisa coming back someday? Would she "wake up" one morning and realize her heart was at home with her husband and their two children? Should he wait for her, avoiding other relationships, in case she suddenly came home?

For Gary, the agony of those years was much worse than the eventual pain of the divorce itself. When he considered dating other women, he felt guilty. When his children asked if their mother would ever return, he didn't know what to say to them. The uncertainty and complexity of his daily life was almost unbearable at times.

He didn't ask for advice, but everyone seemed ready to offer it. The perspective seemed different with every person who advised him. Some told him he should "stay faithful" to his wife, wherever she was. Others told him he was now "free" to "consider other women" if he wished. Gary didn't know what to think—he was busy trying to survive, trying to help his kids survive.

After three years, he began legal action; a divorce was eventually granted. His wife did not contest the filing or seek custody of their children. With his legal and marital status clearly defined, he experienced a welcome sense of closure; the divorce brought him a sense of completion and finality.

■ ■ ■ ■

Until that time, his daily life was about suffering. He gained weight, lost two jobs, and experienced colds and flu that lasted months instead of weeks. His physical health deteriorated; his emotional and mental health similarly waned. Not the type to talk to a pastor or counselor, Gary kept his anxious feelings bottled up inside. He slept fitfully, if at all, racked by worry and doubt.

When he did reach out to seek help (it took him forever, by his own admission) he sought the advice and counsel of his mother and stepdad. Although they were pleasant to him, neither seemed able to offer much that was useful.

"I remember my mom saying something like 'Honey, you're gonna get through this' or words to that effect," Gary says today. "And she meant well, but her saying that didn't help me at all. I didn't believe her—I didn't believe I was going to get through this."

Gary's mother and stepfather did agree to babysit his children at times, freeing him to look for jobs or get projects done around the house. So in that way Gary is definitely grateful for the assistance he received from his family. Yet the help he needed most seemed elusive. He almost quit trying. Then, without warning, he made a reconnection that began to change his life for the better.

"One day I got a note from my birth dad. He just wrote to me out of the blue; he didn't know anything at all about Marisa leaving. He sent me his e-mail address and told me I should write him sometime—he'd like to talk. He said it had been too long since we'd really connected—and if I wanted to, he was ready to talk to me about anything and everything."

Out of that seemingly random connection (Gary still does not know why his birth father wrote at that moment or how it came about) Gary began to develop a sense of affection and respect for the man who had "abandoned him" as a child.

"My dad and I hadn't talked since I was in college," he remembers. "He helped out financially with some of my school bills, but even then we didn't talk much. He offered to give me some money, I thanked him—that was about it."

Gary's father, twice married and twice divorced, seemed an unlikely source of wise information about marriage relationships or how to deal with women. Yet Gary was in no position to judge someone else or to be skeptical about the advice he received—he just needed help. He poured out his feelings to his dad, typing away on the computer after the kids were asleep.

To his amazement, Gary discovered that his dad was wiser than he knew.

"You should wait for her, but not forever," Gary recalls his dad advising. "Everyone deserves a chance to come back, to start over. But you can't just sit there and wait for her forever. Pick a certain amount of time—any amount of time—and wait for her that long. After that, if she's not back, figure out how to start getting a divorce so you can get on with your life."

■ ■ ■ ■

By that time Gary was exchanging messages with his birth father almost daily. Gary was 32. His birth dad, by Gary's estimate, was over 60.

"My kids didn't even know their grandpa," he says today. "They knew my stepdad as Grandpa, and they liked him. But they didn't know my real dad yet; he wasn't there when they were born. He did send them presents, though."

Gary and his father began to develop an open and honest relationship, which Gary believes may have been easier because it was online. "We talked about stuff that maybe we couldn't have talked about face-to-face," he admits. "It was easier because we weren't looking at each other, so we didn't have to hold back or pretend. We could just say how we felt about things."

At one point, Gary told his dad he'd been mad at him for a long time, that he felt like his dad had abandoned him and ignored the whole family. His father's response was surprising.

"Yes, that's how it was," is the way Gary remembers his dad writing back the next day. "I didn't know what else to do at the time. I couldn't make it work with your mother, so I just left."

His dad did not ask to be forgiven, but Gary says it isn't necessary.

"I don't need that," he insists. "I just needed to let him know how I felt. He seemed to handle that okay. I don't need him to say he's sorry, or to beg me for forgiveness. What good would that do? It was a long time ago."

■ ■ ■ ■

Gary and his father began a conversation that continues to this day. Gary credits his dad with the healing and personal growth he began to experience as he moved forward, taking concrete steps to resolve the many problems caused by having an absentee wife and mother.

Most of those problems involved the kids.

"I needed help with parenting stuff," Gary freely admits. "I knew I wasn't the best dad, but at least I loved my kids. Since I was talking to my dad anyway, I started asking him for advice on what to say to my son—how to handle my daughter's fits of anger, which were constant.

"I know it sounds crazy to ask a runaway dad for advice about parenting, but at the time it seemed like the natural thing to do.

We were talking so much anyway. My dad had some really good advice about getting control of Alicia's temper—what he told me to try was the first thing that had worked in a long time."

At what Gary describes as "the lowest point in my life" he discovered his own support network.

At his father's suggestion, Gary began sending the kids to be with his mother and stepdad one night per week, at a regular time and on a consistent schedule. Gary's mom and stepdad seemed to enjoy being helpful; they also appreciated the regularity of knowing that every Friday night, they would have their two grandkids. It helped them plan and organize their own weekly routines.

Friday nights became "Gary time" so that Gary could take a class, go out with his friends, get some work done around the house, or just sleep. "I took a lot of Friday evening naps," he says with a sheepish grin. "The exciting life of a single parent! I was so worn out after a week of working and coming home to care for my kids. I was exhausted most of the time."

Gary became closer to his mom and stepdad; closer also to his birth dad, who lived several hundred miles away in another state. Both of these family relationships helped him adjust and cope. His mother provided a steady and regular night of child care (sometimes overnight if needed), while his birth father provided advice, encouragement, and moral support. Enough time had passed since his parents divorced that his mother and father, while not in frequent contact with each other, were at least cordial, social, and peaceful.

"I've never needed my parents as much as I did in those first few years," Gary tells us today. "All three of them helped us get through it: my dad, my stepdad, and my mom. All three of them can take credit for how my kids are turning out, how my life is turning out. They really helped me figure out what to do next, how to deal with the unfairness of the whole thing."

At what Gary describes as "the lowest point in my life" he discovered his own support network of caring older adults who were willing to help. Each helped in different ways, as he or she was able. Each one contributed to Gary's health. Each one became a partner in Gary's recovery from depression and worry.

Reaching Out to Build Your Network

In the pain and trauma that accompany a divorce or abandonment, you may often feel as though you're entirely alone. You may withdraw from social contact, isolate yourself from friends, and lose interest in doing things that you once enjoyed, such as going to movies or out to dinner.

These are normal responses to feelings of rejection. Yet they are also dangerous patterns for a single parent to establish. The truth is, you will need your family and friends around you in the days and weeks after a separation or divorce. It will be vitally important to hear different perspectives, receive well-intentioned advice, and perhaps even benefit from some financial help. The thing you least want to do—be around people—may be one of the most helpful steps you can take on the long journey toward personal health.

It's important for you to listen to other perspectives, and it is equally important for your family and close friends to know how you're doing. There is no point in pretending that "everything's okay" when you are depressed, angry, and feeling more alone than you've ever felt in your life. Talk to a counselor, a pastor, a co-worker, or a friend. Talk to your brothers and sisters, your parents and stepparents. Let people know what your needs are.

Since your friends will probably have opinions anyway, go ahead and ask. Show respect for what you hear, though it isn't necessary to agree. Avoid arguing—why alienate the people who haven't left you? It's time to value your friendships and your family connections more than ever before.

It is typical for a stressed-out single parent, before or after the divorce becomes final, to underestimate the strength and compassion that exist in her or his family circle. Often a single parent fails to ask anyone for much-needed help, believing that meaningful help is not available anyway. It is not uncommon for a single parent to prejudge others as unwilling or unable to help.

"My family doesn't have any money," sighed one single parent. "There's no point in going there."

By deciding in advance that her parents were not able to assist her financially, this busy mom missed opportunities to receive whatever care her parents might have offered. Insisting on going it alone, she cut herself off from resources that may have been available to her—and more importantly, to her children as well.

No one likes to be dependent on others for emotional support or financial aid. In the long run, becoming dependent will weaken your self-esteem and prove to be counterproductive. Yet in the early days of single parenting, many adults are so anxious to avoid seeming dependent that they hide the truth from people who not only care, but are ready and able to help.

Staying Away from the Victim Mentality

Grace was surprised by an unexpected response from her older sister.

"My sister was on her second marriage, and it was working really well," she recalls. "When my husband left me I was desperately afraid. I had no idea how I was going to support my kids and keep the household together. I didn't want to talk about it; I really didn't want to face it.

"My sister Emily sat down with me and asked point-blank questions about my debts, my monthly payments, my expenses, everything. I mean, we had never had that kind of conversation before—those things are so personal. But I told her how things were, and she made written notes while we talked.

"The next thing I knew, Emily's husband was handing me a check. He told me it wasn't a loan, it was a gift. He also told me that if they could, he and my sister would provide other gifts from time to time. He told me not to worry, that I was going to get through this and become a stronger person.

"When he told me not to worry, it was such a big encouragement to me. After that conversation I started believing there might be a way to hang on."

Grace had been busy in her own marriage, raising her young children. She had not really gotten close to her sister's new husband. Her relationship with her sister had been occasional and casual, not constant and deep. Yet in the midst of her most difficult crisis, she received a check that covered a month's rent, her car payment, her car-insurance payment—and more than $500 beyond that sum.

Grace was stunned to discover that her sister and brother-in-law could afford to help in such a generous way. "They aren't wealthy," she insists. "They don't drive a new car or live in a big house. I thought they were barely getting by!"

In the first 18 months after her husband left her, Grace received four more checks from her sister and brother-in-law.

"I don't know the exact figure," she confides, "but I know they gave me more than $10,000 in about a year-and-a-half. That's such a big amount of money, and we needed it so desperately! It made all the difference for us, helping us get through that time after Jack left."

Although others were also helpful to Grace and her children, it was the caring involvement of an older sister—herself having been through a divorce—that brought Grace through the valleys and dark places in the months immediately after her husband was gone. Her sister was matter-of-fact, calm, optimistic, and very generous with money. Grace hopes to be of similar value to others, when they experience the suffering she faced.

"I hope I'm able to do for someone else what my sister and Steve were able to do for me. It might not be the same dollar amount, but if I'm able to help another single mom get through those tough first months, I would love to do it," she says with an open smile. "I'll never forget what it felt like to be so down, so depressed, to feel like there just weren't any options or any answers."

■ ■ ■ ■

Single parents often feel this way. Single dads may feel completely unqualified to nurture and care for their children, particularly younger ones. Single mothers may have limited exposure to financial realities, and may find themselves with a dusty job résumé and few prospects for a well-paying job. In spite of these feelings—which are normal and common—it's important for single parents to reach out to family members and others, beginning to build a network of social interaction and emotional support.

Doing so is not about building an "I hate Alex!" group, in which everyone contributes negative comments about an ex-partner. Anger and resentment directed against others may provide temporary emotional relief, but they are not helpful in the longer term. An effective support group should be prepared to affirm, build up, and encourage a single parent, helping the now-single adult see herself as capable and strong, rather than as a suffering "victim."

"The victim mentality is a huge trap for single parents," says one busy counselor, a woman who sees a dozen or more single parents among her regular weekly clients. "It's so easy to fall into the trap of feeling sorry for yourself, getting stuck in how unfair life has been. Although it's natural to feel like that, it's also a complete dead end. It doesn't take you anywhere useful."

Although it's normal to feel like a victim of unfair circumstances— a feeling that may be rooted in actual fact—the process of moving forward begins with taking control of your thoughts, attitudes, and emotions and accepting responsibility for your own future. As you do so, one of the most powerful tools to assist your personal journey is a support network of caring family members who will cheer for you and encourage you in the midst of your many new challenges.

Finding Optimism and Good Advice

Dorothy's support network included an elderly aunt, herself a divorced woman who had outlived a second husband after a lengthy remarriage. Although this aunt had been a single parent more than 30 years earlier, the issues were surprisingly similar to those that Dorothy faced.

"She knew exactly what I was feeling," Dorothy says about her aunt. "Although my mom was great during that whole time, it was

Aunt Betty who counseled me to keep getting out of bed in the morning, keep doing my best for the kids, and keep believing that a good job was out there waiting for me.

"Aunt Betty wasn't just being cheerful or optimistic. She had been through the exact same problems I was going through, and at a time when women were not so involved in the workplace. So if anything, she may have had a harder life than I did, after she got divorced."

Dorothy paid attention to her aunt's admonitions, often relying on her strong positive energy to keep her own hopes alive. Besides her aunt and her mom and dad, Dorothy's primary support network included an older brother, who was still single in his mid-40s.

"Frank kept telling me not to give up on men," she recalls. "He kept telling me not to think badly of all men everywhere just because my ex had run away from his problems, leaving me to do all the hard work. I needed to hear that, because I was pretty angry at men in general those first few years."

Dorothy did not receive financial help from anyone in her support network and admits she did not ask for any.

"That's not how I am," she says succinctly. "I make my own way."

Yet although she did not seek or receive financial assistance, she both asked for and benefited from the emotional support, wise counsel, and comforting presence of her family members. Their value to her transcended dollar amounts and cannot be measured in a quantitative way.

"They got me through all this," Dorothy says simply. "Aunt Betty especially, but all of them got me through it. They never let me take the easy way out; they never let me sit around feeling sorry for myself all day. Without Frank, Aunt Betty, and Mom and Dad, I don't know where I'd be today, and I don't know where my kids would be."

Eight years into her journey of single parenting, Dorothy now has a son in his first year of college.

"He's an honor student," Dorothy boasts. "When his dad left, Mike took it harder than the other kids. He was angry, withdrawn, upset, and didn't want to talk about it. I worried about him during middle school and in his early high-school years. But somehow today he's back to being his usual high-achiever self. He got a good scholarship (to Stanford) and he's keeping his grades up."

We tell Dorothy she must have done something right as a single mom.

"I didn't do it alone," she shoots back. "There's no way any human being can be both a mother and a father to young kids. I did my best and I believe God helped our family get through this. But I also believe that my family helped me—helped all of us—come through some really rough days."

■ ■ ■ ■

When family members support a single parent in the right ways—with sturdy but genuine optimism, with respectful and low-key advice, the effect is to create a growing sense of competency and well-being within the struggling adult. Over time, a sense of competency may be one of the most useful tools the support network can pass along to a single mother or father trying to cope with being alone, raising a family, and making a living.

Although traditional studies suggest that a man's self-esteem is linked to his role as provider and guardian, it appears that single parents of both sexes are boosted by working and earning income. Few external factors and circumstances are more helpful to the confidence level of a single parent than having a good-paying job that provides a firm financial foundation for the family.

Here again, a support network of caring family members may prove useful in searching for jobs, helping to acquire needed training, or providing child care during the education or employment of a single parent. One single parent we interviewed found employment through the efforts of her father, who had retired from a major corporation. With a few phone calls, the father was able to uncover some job openings that had not yet been posted, giving his suddenly single daughter the chance to polish her résumé for a role that would soon be open. She was able to get an interview quickly and was hired shortly thereafter.

Never underestimate the power and influence of your network.

Getting Much and Giving Back

Overwhelmed by their own needs in many areas, including child care and money struggles, single parents often feel as though they're on the "receiving end" in many relationships. A woman of good conscience may not be comfortable in the role of being only a receiver. If you find yourself feeling that way—that you're doing "too much receiving"—look for ways to give back to those who are helping you. Or search for effective and useful ways to help others.

As you receive the gracious help of family and friends, it is important that you not feel deeply obligated or indebted to those who assist you. Flee from people who seek to use their financial gifts to gain some kind of leverage in your life and your choices, people who obviously want something in return for their offers of help. Such help may come at too high a price.

If your parents are helping you financially, look for ways you and your children can provide "free labor" for much-needed chores around your parents' home. Cut the grass, shovel the sidewalk, rake the leaves, or offer to clean out the garage. These services provide tangible and direct benefits to your parents or others, particularly if your parents are older or retired. Offer to do these things from an attitude of cheerful helping, not because you feel it is your duty.

An added advantage of this behavior is teaching your children about giving to others, showing your children that hard work while helping others is a powerful way to gain self-confidence and self-esteem. Once again, provide these services without feeling obligated or indebted. Rather, help out with gladness and gratitude—grateful for what you have received, and glad that you can to some extent give back to those who have been so helpful to you.

One single parent regularly bakes cookies with her children, distributing the results among her support network of family and friends. Since her kids are still young, the cookies are often misshapen, over-baked, and "creative." The busy single mom is learning that her friends and family appreciate the uniqueness of these thoughtful gifts—in a world of store-bought uniformity, cookies baked and frosted by young children provide a welcome breath of originality.

As you explore these options, be careful not to take away the blessings of those who are giving to you. If every gift you receive triggers an immediate countergift, you may be diminishing the satisfaction and joy received by those who only wish to help. Learn to be a gracious receiver—an art in itself—and if you can occasionally give back in some way, do so happily.

> Learn to be a gracious receiver... and if you can occasionally give back in some way, do so happily.

Single parenting is a season, even if the season lasts a decade or more. Each of us will experience seasons in which we receive—because we are in need. Hopefully each of us will also experience seasons in which our generosity and our resources allow us to bless others by giving.

As a stressed, depressed, sometimes-overwhelmed single parent, accept a season of receiving as a chance to be blessed by others. Build a support network that includes family members and friends. Allow your parents, siblings, or other relatives to offer you their advice, their help with child care, or their financial aid.

Bear in mind that most of this help is temporary. Your kids will get older and go to school; the depth of your financial need will ebb somewhat. Rather than feeling dependent and unworthy, recognize the fact that your circumstances allow a family (or a group of friends) to function at its best: helping those within the circle who genuinely need the help and assistance.

■ ■ ■ ■

As the seasons of life unfold, most of us will experience need along the way.

Families are intended to be places where members help each other, bearing each other's burdens and supporting each other. Your proper place in a family will involve both giving and receiving, both having need and giving generously.

If your financial needs are extreme today, allow yourself a moment to realize that in the future, you may have the joy of giving to others. Promise yourself to help others when you are able—then experience the joy of keeping that promise when it becomes possible.

3

The Role of Community
in Raising Your Children

■ ■ ■ ■

It takes a village to raise a child.

AFRICAN PROVERB

Danae was 23 when she learned she would become a single parent. She was not married; the father of her child was a boyfriend she had known for only a few months. Danae's "boyfriend" ended the relationship before learning of her pregnancy. She considered telling him about it after the fact, but decided that he had already made his choice—he had left her.

Her inner circle included four close friends from college, all of whom had remained in their college town, gotten jobs, and stayed connected. When she learned she was pregnant, Danae immediately informed these key friends.

Their reaction surprised her.

"One of my closest girlfriends suggested an abortion immediately," she says, still seeming shocked by this advice. "I totally did not expect that! I thought we all had the same values, we were all basically Christians with the same views."

This particular girlfriend not only suggested that Danae have an abortion, she further insisted that she "not wait" since the baby would keep on growing if she took time to make up her mind.

Danae didn't need any time.

"I only had two choices, really," she declares. "To give away my child, or keep it and become a single mom. I would never kill my own baby."

Single, with many thousands of dollars to pay in student loans, Danae couldn't see how pregnancy would fit with her plans for the future. She seriously and prayerfully considered planning an adoption, a choice she respects and nearly selected.

Yet by about the fifth month of her term, Danae knew for sure that she would keep her child, regardless of the cost or the consequences. "I knew this baby was a part of me, and I was a part of her," she shares. "I also knew I wanted us to stay together, even if it wasn't easy."

A Circle of Friends

Once Danae revealed her final decision, all four of her friends rallied to her cause, including the one who had recommended abortion. Danae was rooming with two of the women; the other two roomed together and lived nearby.

Her first thought was that, while she was pregnant and definitely during her daughter's infancy, she would need to move out and find a new place to rent. Her roommates had other ideas and told her so.

"You're staying right here, both of you," Danae recalls her friends telling her. "You can't afford a place of your own. We'll buy earplugs if we need to, we'll keep our bedroom doors tightly shut or whatever it takes, but we want you and your daughter living right here with us. Don't even think of moving out!" Both of Danae's roommates made these statements; each one seemed sincere and genuine.

She was shocked but felt blessed—having done the math already, she knew she couldn't easily afford a place on her own. After checking to make certain that her roommates were serious, Danae accepted their offer. Carefully rearranging her own bedroom, she made space for a crib in one corner. Meanwhile, her girlfriends began buying her baby clothes and accessories.

When the baby came, one of her roommates drove her to the

hospital (the other one was working), and within an hour of the birth, all four of her girlfriends were at her side supporting and congratulating her.

"We all crowded into the birthing room," Danae recounts. "It was fixed up almost like a bedroom in a house. After the nurse was finished with measuring, all my friends started passing my baby around the room. I almost didn't get to hold her myself! I had to ask to get her back."

This idyllic scene did not mean Danae's life would be stress-free. On the contrary, her daughter, Emma, proved a light sleeper, a frequent waker, and a hungry baby who wanted feedings at irregular hours. The demands of the new schedule were experienced not only by Danae, but by her roommates as well.

"One of my roommates was engaged," Danae smiles. "And maybe when I had my baby, they hurried up their timetable a little bit. I think they might have moved up the wedding date a few months so Kerri could get out of the house."

■ ■ ■ ■

In spite of the noise and hassles, the group of friends pulled together and took turns doing child care. Each of the two friends who lived in a different apartment building was a frequent visitor to Danae's home. They watched Emma in the evenings from time to time so that Danae could hopefully "crash" and try to catch up on much-needed sleep. Meanwhile, her two roommates also took turns watching her daughter, rocking the baby to sleep, and warming formula on the stove.

We ask Danae about her stress level during her daughter's first few months of life. We also inquire about fighting or arguments among the roommates during those early weeks and months.

"It's weird," she says, considering her words. "I think we fought less during that time, not more. It was like we all pulled together, because there was a big important reason to pull together. So even though we were sleeping less—every one of us in that apartment was sleeping less—and even though it was tense and tough at times, I think we fought less than we would have otherwise."

Even so, Danae wishes she'd had a husband. "But I wasn't exactly at my 'prime dating moment' during the pregnancy and for that first year afterward. I was a sleep-deprived zombie a lot of the time. I held on to a part-time job, juggled day care around my schedule and my friends' schedules—I didn't exactly have time for a social life, and I really wasn't in the mood for one anyway."

Today, with Emma a few months away from starting pre-K, Danae is beginning to think about dating. She's been seeing a guy for a few months, a guy she considers a "friend" rather than "boyfriend," but she's ready to consider taking the relationship to the next level.

"I'm okay with dating him, if it turns out that way," she claims. "And I'm also okay if it stays like it is. We're friends, we do things together, he's good with Emma. I watch him play with my daughter and I think to myself—*Yes, he could be a father to her someday.* But we'll see how things work out."

Of the original five college friends, two are now married. One of the married friends has given birth, an experience Danae was prepared to guide and help her friend understand. "She wanted to know everything," Danae remembers. "And for once I got to be the expert about something."

Married or single, parents or not, the five friends continue to find common ground based on their shared life experiences in college and beyond. "It's like Emma has four aunts or four extra mothers," Danae smiles. "She's being raised by a lot of people that really care about her. It's nice to have people in my life I totally trust—if any of my friends are watching Emma, I know she's okay."

Danae's friends form a useful "village" as she raises her daughter. Although Danae is a single parent, she is definitely not alone as she faces the challenges of raising her daughter. The birth of her child—which might have isolated her from her primary social network—has instead bonded the friends together in new ways, drawing the circle even tighter than it was before.

The Corporation as Community

Can a single mom find useful help where she least expects it—at work? Can a single father juggle the demands of keeping a job and raising his kids?

As the Internet continues to reshape and redefine our global economy, options such as telecommuting, paternity leave, and flex-time make it possible for working parents to balance the needs of family and employment. No one struggles more intensely with these issues than single parents; helpfully, though, many large companies are putting family-friendly policies in place.

Each year, various organizations evaluate the United States corporate community looking for the "best places to work." They review companies—typically large organizations employing hundreds or thousands of people—then announce their findings. When they are reviewing a corporation during this process, family-friendly policies are often a key measure of its becoming a "best place."

An organization called Working Mother regularly surveys America's corporations in search of the best companies for working moms. Each year the group releases its "Top 100" list and also a related "Top 10" list of employers whose care for their employees includes family-friendly benefits and policies. Companies are carefully screened with regard to the services they provide and the benefits they offer for busy working women with children.

For example, the SC Johnson company recently made the Working Mother "Top 10" list with employee benefits that include an in-house doctor and on-site child care. The vice president of global public affairs and communication, Kelley Semrau, shares the fact that she uses the company's on-site day care for her two children, ages five and two. She has also consulted the in-house doctor about treatments that a family member is considering while coping with cancer. Further, SC Johnson also offers an in-house store—so if Kelly needs to buy milk on the way home, she can pick it up at work before she leaves.

SC Johnson's policies are generous for men as well as working mothers. Recently two men in the communications office received paid paternity leave so they could be at home with their families while welcoming new additions.

Enlightened practices such as these are increasingly changing the landscape of American employment in ways that are single-parent-friendly. Imagine being a single mom and having a doctor, a child-care provider, and a grocery store all under your employer's roof!

Talk about one-stop shopping—in an era of high and rapidly rising gas prices, it is incredibly convenient to drop off the kids, pick up the groceries, and consult for medical advice in the same building where you work.

■ ■ ■ ■

CIGNA recently made the Working Mother "Top 100" list for the ninth straight year. The company established 3000 new tele-commuting work-at-home arrangements within one year. In some cases, the company believes these flexible arrangements save as much as an hour a day in commuting time, yielding almost 30 days of extra personal time per year for each of these valuable and respected employees.

Donald Levinson, executive vice president of human resources at CIGNA, comments, "We are truly honored to be recognized once again as one of the best companies for working mothers. CIGNA works hard to develop workplace programs to help women find balance and success in their business and personal lives. Our programs have proven time and time again to be a great way to enable people to be their best—both at home and at work."

CIGNA's innovative family-friendly programs include telecommuting, job-sharing, on-site child care, on-site health care, take-home meal services, and nursing mothers' rooms.

The rest of corporate America is taking notice and making changes as more and more major companies lead the way in family-friendly practices.

Mark Loughridge, father of six, serves as senior vice president and chief financial officer for IBM. "We view worklife programs as tools to achieve business results, not as barriers or obligations we must provide," Loughridge declares. IBM has made the "100 Best" list for working mothers for 20 years.

Rounding out the list are numerous other companies, whose locations span the country from east to west and from north to south. Although usually located in major cities rather than rural areas, the policies established by North America's larger businesses serve as examples for corporations of all sizes, with many of the best practices becoming templates that transform even smaller companies into family-friendly places to work.

> Friendships formed in the workplace can and often do assume the roles served by an extended family network in previous generations.

Single parents are increasingly savvy about these options; more than half of the single parents we interviewed for this project mentioned working at home as one of the top goals they'd love to achieve. In addition to seeking good health-care coverage, single parents continue to seek employers who recognize that, as important as the job is, it is also important to have a balanced family life.

Another dimension of the workplace experience is that working in an office or factory can produce a network of friends who support and encourage a single mom or dad in their difficult challenges. For some single parents, the closest friends they have—the people they know the best and who know them the most completely—are friends from the office. As the increasingly high mobility of our society results in college graduates taking jobs far away from their families, friendships formed in the workplace can and often do assume the roles served by an extended family network in previous generations.

The Community Within the Congregation

Another source of key supportive relationships can be found within many communities of faith. Caring members of churches, synagogues, and temples are typically attentive and proactive in seeking ways to serve and help single parents.

In a smaller church setting, the congregation may literally take on the roles and functions of a family group, surrounding the single parent and her children with care, counsel, encouragement, and even financial support. Children may grow up becoming closer to a circle of friends at church than they are to their own biological relatives. Children experience role models among older children, teens, adults—including married adults—and senior citizens.

Larger church settings may not provide the same depth or intensity of relationships, yet may often sponsor programs and ministries that target single dads and moms with many useful services—including child care, home and yard maintenance, "Mom's Night Out" or "Mom's Day Off" activities, and more. What larger churches lack in personal closeness, they often make up in the sheer volume of care and options they can provide.

Single parents find many benefits among congregations of all sizes.

"My boys have a bunch of aunts and uncles, a ton of grandparents," Kara insists, describing the church (150 in average weekly attendance) that she calls her spiritual home. "My sons are growing up knowing they're loved, not just by me but by a whole bunch of people of all different ages. It's like we're part of one big family together. Everyone cares, everyone helps."

■ ■ ■ ■

Adele has a similar perspective about her small group, one of literally hundreds of small groups that meet weekly in her large suburban congregation. "The couples in my small group know exactly what I'm going through," she says. "I may be the only single parent in the group, but I've never felt like I was different, or left out, or alone. Really, parenting is parenting—I'm constantly getting good advice from other moms and dads about how to handle my sons."

We ask Adele what her church offers her in terms of support.

"We just had a divorce-recovery seminar. They do that two or three times a year. It didn't really matter to me until I got divorced—all of a sudden, I was really glad our church has this ministry!

"We spent a Saturday morning together, a whole group of newly divorced people and a few that have been divorced for quite a while. It was kind of like group therapy in a good way. Our guest speakers didn't just talk; they asked us questions about how we felt, what we were going through."

Adele was surprised by the depth and intimacy of the answers. "After the first hour, I'd already heard things I couldn't believe people would openly share and admit. And by the end of the second hour, I think most of us had shared at that level. Before the morning was over, we realized we were all human, we were all imperfect—and we also realized that God loves us and that His grace reaches us right where we live."

Adele credits the guest speakers with creating an open, nonthreatening atmosphere in which people felt free to share.

"We were mostly women," Adele explains. "But there were men too. Frankly I wasn't sure that having men and women together in the same divorce-recovery seminar was such a good idea. But I found myself relating to what the men were going through, and the men seemed to understand what we felt like as women. I guess maybe divorce gives people a lot in common, men or women."

Adele's large church uses the Saturday-morning divorce-recovery seminars as kickoff events for small-group sessions that last from six to ten weeks, depending on the topics. These small groups are different from the regular small groups that meet weekly in the broader congregation. The divorce groups watch video presentations, receive homework assignments, and meet weekly to process the information they learn about how to manage money, how to raise children, how to deal with difficult ex-spouses, and more.

"I've been to the seminars twice now," Adele says, smiling. "And the second time it was mostly the same information as the first time, but I needed it all over again. I was surprised how much I learned when I went back the second time. Honestly, I think I'll go back again—and I'll bet I hear things that seem new to me even on my third try."

She has been to only one of the small-group courses, yet she found it helpful and timely. "It's hard for me to commit to a one-night-a-week class, even if it's only for six weeks," Adele laments. "I missed one session of the class that I attended, but I enjoyed the rest of them. I wasn't convinced that sitting around watching a video was going to change my life—but when I got there, the things the speaker on the video was talking about were exactly what I needed to know."

■■■■

If you live in a major city within driving distance of a megachurch, consider visiting the Web site or campus of the congregation. You need not abandon your own house of worship—simply check out the resources and opportunities that are offered for single parents, divorced persons, or those who are considering remarriage. You may be amazed at the variety of classes, retreats, seminars, and conferences that are hosted or supported by larger churches.

While maintaining your attendance at and support of the local church you already call home, you may be able to take classes or catch a Saturday-morning seminar that provides exactly the help and information you need as a newly divorced woman or as a stressed-out single dad. Sign up for e-mail newsletters and other sources of ongoing information for single parents.

Large communities of faith can be remarkably supportive places for divorced persons and single parents to network with others who are undergoing similar challenges, setbacks, and difficulties. A single mother who feels "different" in a small church with its tightly knit intact families may discover she is "much the same" as many others within a larger congregation.

Again, it is not necessary to abandon your own preferred house of worship in order to take advantage of classes and conferences at larger churches. If you don't know which churches to consider, begin by asking others or searching the Internet for nearby options.

At Adele's church, the divorce-recovery seminars include a feature that Adele greatly appreciates: free child care for the entire morning. For Adele, that feature was the deal-clincher.

"The seminar itself isn't free, but the price is surprisingly low," she says of the Saturday-morning events. "Once you get there, there's free coffee and also usually free muffins, cake, or cookies. The free child care is such a lifesaver; that is literally why I signed up the first time. I wanted to come, but I didn't want to ask someone to give up their Saturday to watch my boys. So when I found out the child care was free, I brought the kids along. So far—I've been to two seminars—I've never had to leave a session to deal with a problem with my kids."

When she signed up for the second seminar, she brought two other single moms along with her. "I'd been telling them about it for months," Adele laughs. "And it's not like I gave them an option. I told them, 'You're coming with me the next time this happens!' and for some reason they did come with me."

Adele, though not currently seeing a counselor at the church, keeps in touch with two of the women therapists who serve in the church's large counseling center.

"Mary just told me that the church is thinking about hiring a pastor for divorced people or stepfamilies," Adele relates. "And when they were talking about it, the idea of having a pastor for single parents also came up. So who knows? Someday soon there may be a pastor on staff here just for people going through divorce, or just for those of us who are single parents."

In a nation where 1300 new stepfamilies are formed daily, and in which more than 2 million adults divorce each year—some of them for a second time—churches are wise to consider adding staff members whose ministry focuses on this large and growing segment of society. Instead of lagging behind cultural trends, many contemporary churches are attempting to get out in front and lead by innovation, meeting needs where they find them.

Meanwhile, communities of faith of all sizes continue to explore ways to better serve those whose marriages have ended, including those who are busy trying to raise children alone.

■ ■ ■ ■

If you are stressed out and feeling isolated in your challenging role as a single dad or mom, help may be closer to home than you realize. Whether you turn to a circle of friends, an enlightened employer, a network of acquaintances in your workplace, or a caring congregation, finding your place within a broader community can be healthy for you and for your children. Connect where you can, and discover the blessings of sharing within a "village" near you.

4

Taking Care of Yourself

Physical Health
and Wellness

■ ■ ■ ■

*I caught a cold about a month after
my divorce became final. That was 18 months
ago, and I'm still sneezing.*

TABITHA, SINGLE MOTHER, AGE 26

In the first three chapters of this part of the book, we've looked at faith, family, and community, exploring the ways in which these activities and connections can nourish and sustain you, helping you through one of the most difficult times of your entire life. Each of these three categories involves circumstances outside of your own control, yet each one also leaves you with personal responsibility: explore your faith; allow your family to be meaningfully involved in your life; connect with a caring community on the job, at church, or among your friends.

In this chapter we'll consider an area that is more directly under your personal authority and responsibility—your physical health and wellness. As you read the ideas and insights in this chapter, allow your love for your children to motivate you to start taking better care of yourself.

The Health-Smart Reasons to Rest

Stressed out and challenged by caring for young children, single parents are among the most underrested adults of any demographic category. Both men and women report that their patterns of sleep and rest change radically after the experience of a divorce, more so for the parent with primary or sole custody.

Single fathers often report late-night anxiety attacks, sleeplessness, and loss of interest in eating. Single mothers frequently mention irregular schedules, infants waking them through the night, and a wearying fatigue that leaves them tired but somehow still unable to get to sleep. Single parents of both sexes seem remarkably prone to sleep deprivation and the lack of restorative downtime.

Divorce—in and of itself—stresses the body's immune system, weakening your natural defenses against disease and illness. Studies now coming to light suggest significant linkage between the onset of many major illnesses, such as various types of cancer, and the recent experience of a traumatic event such as divorce or the loss of a relationship.

It appears that there may be "trigger events" that detonate a high level of stress throughout a person's immune system, slowing or reducing the body's innate ability to ward off infection and serious illness. We may soon discover that the onset of abnormal cell growth (cancers fit within this broad category) is often preceded by highly stressful events or situations, including the loss of a job, the death of a parent, partner, or child, or the breakup of a marriage and family.

To be certain, the trauma of divorce is an event of this magnitude. For the children involved, for the two adults, and for close family members and friends, separation and divorce can lead to anxiety, depression, anger, and fear. Fallout from the trauma can linger for years and even decades—adult children of divorce often report they are still processing issues and problems from 20, 30, or more years ago. Divorce is one of the most significant stressors yet identified in the emerging study of the links between trauma and serious illness.

Meanwhile, in addition to the impact of stress on their immune systems, single parents face yet another threat to their body's natural defenses: lack of rest. As we travel throughout North America and beyond, single parents continue to make up one of the most sleep-deprived groups among any of those we meet.

Jeanette, a single mom in her early 30s, is a prime example. She grimaces when we advise her to get more rest, wrinkling her face as if we've suggested the impossible. Her words confirm this diagnosis.

"How can I possibly get any rest?" she wants to know. "My nine-month-old is keeping me awake all night, and the other two are chasing me around the house all day! I haven't slept well for the past year!"

If you're a busy single parent, particularly if you have a child under 12 months of age or have several children younger than school age,

> The...likely reason for these ailments is that they are chronically underrested.

you may feel exactly like Jeanette does: Even if rest is important, how can you possibly make it happen? Rest seems out of the question for many single parents, especially those with infants.

■ ■ ■ ■

Before we talk in detail about getting enough rest, let's look at why it's so vitally important. Study after study confirms a direct link between getting enough rest—particularly the renewing stages of REM time (rapid eye movement during the deepest part of sleep)—and your body's ability to fight infections, resist germs, and do battle with viruses.

At the heart of one of today's great medical challenges—the AIDS crisis—are two words: *immune deficiency.* Those who are suffering from AIDS in its later stages generally die of some other malady. AIDS strikes, weakens, and destroys the body's immune system, leaving it unable to attack and defeat invasive diseases. And one of these other diseases—which invades the body after AIDS weakens or destroys the immune system—is often the cause of death.

Although you may not be at risk for AIDS, many single parents do fall into the category of persons who have lowered and somewhat deficient immune systems. Their ability to ward off viruses and infections is often greatly reduced.

The reason is simple: Parents of young children, and especially single parents, often don't get enough physical rest to keep their immune systems functioning at their highest and best capacity. This is why so many single parents report coughs, colds, sneezing, sore throats, chronic headaches, and many other physical ailments that not only impair their health, but linger for long periods of times.

Single parents often report coughs or colds that have lasted for months at a time. Others admit to constant fatigue, headaches, and other recurring physical ills. Busy single moms and dads tend to tell us that they "picked up a bug" or "got it from the kids," when the more likely reason for these ailments is that they are chronically underrested.

How to Get the Rest You Need:
Lessons from Other Single Parents

As a stressed-out single parent, how do you begin to get enough rest? Here's a look at some real-life remedies suggested by other single mothers and fathers who are finding pathways to personal health.

1. Nap in the afternoons. Even if this has never been your usual habit or established pattern, make an effort to begin and continue this helpful practice. After you put the kids down for a nap (all of them!) retire to your own room and try to sleep. Turn off the lights, close the draperies, put soft music on the stereo—these changes to your household environment tend to create a more relaxing atmosphere. If you find that you're not falling asleep, simply lie still and rest with your eyes closed. Force yourself to do nothing at all; cease from physical and mental activity as you rest quietly on a sofa, bed, or favorite chair.

2. When you finally settle down to sleep in the evening, empty your mind of all your worries, cares, and problems. This is not a time to plan out tomorrow's activities or wonder where your next paycheck is coming from. This is not the right moment to reflect about how to change or adjust your child's behavior. Rather, the process of lying down for a nap or a good night's sleep should begin with a decision on your part to clear your mind of all worry, anxiety, and stress.

3. Read the Scriptures—particularly the Psalms—or read a daily devotional book that you find helpful. This is not a time to read for learning or to gain information about how to solve problems—save those educational books for other moments. This is a time for quiet reflection, for contemplative reading that inspires you—even if you scan only a verse or two. If you choose to have a prayer time in the evening, this is not the best hour of the day for long, laborious intercessory prayers about serious problems. Rather, let your pre-resting prayers be moments of gratitude and thanks, counting your blessings, expressing your love to God in your own words and your own way.

4. Try using relaxing music to provide a soothing environment for your children and also for you. Among the best specific suggestions we've received from single parents is the CD *Golden Slumber* by Dave Koz and other artists. This is a collection of traditional and contemporary lullabies adapted for smooth jazz. Even if you prefer classic rock, contemporary worship songs, or other "lively" forms of music, choose relaxing sounds as you prepare to sleep. Quiet music helps you relax at a subconscious level, without distraction. An older cassette tape often recommended by single parents is *Sleep Sound in Jesus* by Michael Card.

5. Develop a consistent bedtime routine and stick to it, regardless of the many obstacles you will face. This is often a hugely difficult step for single parents—many single parents insist this is completely impossible for them.

Later, after they've tried it and decided to keep trying it, these same parents tell us the system works—having a bedtime routine is a great way to condition children about what to expect next. Put away clothes, stow the toys, brush the teeth, say the prayers, tell a story, put on the music...whatever your particular routine involves, it should be repeated and consistent.

If a child learns that he or she can successfully disrupt the routine and thus postpone bedtime, you can be sure of what that child will do: disrupt the routine. Yet if the same child learns that Mom or Dad is serious about the routine—and sticks with it—the very routine itself becomes a form of comfort to the child.

The consistency of regular routine provides a calming daily reassurance that "all is well" and "everything is normal"—hugely valuable for all children, but especially for kids undergoing the stress of trauma and change in their family life. Your children may not thank you for making the change to a structured routine, but persevere anyway. Like many of the approaches you take as you raise your kids, this one is "for their own good"—and as an added benefit, it will help create the time and space you need for personal rest and recovery.

Diet and Nutrition

Not surprisingly, single parents report some of the worst eating habits of any category of adults we work with. There are many plausible explanations for this—you may have rationalized your own bad habits as "rewards" for the stress you're experiencing, or as a coping mechanism for all your worries.

Speaking in general, single parents do not make healthy choices in their personal diet and nutrition. They tend to be careful in what they allow or recommend for their children; this helpful attitude does not seem to apply to self-care.

Single dads tell us they eat a lot of cereal. In fact, we're beginning to wonder if single fathers are the largest category of consumers of cereal products! The cereal-crunching single dad is becoming a cliché of modern adult life.

Is cereal unhealthy? Not at all—in fact, it's becoming a healthier choice almost every day. Major producers are switching to whole-grain flour; in general they are putting much less sugar into their products. A bowl of whole-grain cereal is high in fiber and can be a healthy choice; more so if you add in some fresh fruit and choose fat-free or skim milk. Read your cereal labels and look for whole-grain products that are reasonably low in calories and sodium.

The problem isn't that cereal is a bad choice (chosen wisely), but rather that eating cereal 24/7 is not exactly a balanced diet for you or your kids. Growing children need protein, vitamins, some fat, and beneficial carbohydrates. Your kids should be eating their fruits and vegetables, and so should you. Yet single dads tell us they often opt for "the easy way out" when feeding their children.

Speaking of "easy," quick-cooking macaroni and cheese is another staple of single-parent life, particularly for single dads. As an accompaniment to a meal that includes lean meat, fresh vegetables, and healthy whole-grain breads, there is nothing truly sinister about macaroni and cheese. That said, have you checked the sodium content of most packaged varieties? Living on a steady diet of mac and cheese (with or without chopped-up hot dogs in the mix) does not provide you or your children with balanced nutrition. The high levels of sodium are particularly unhelpful for many adults. As an option or a side dish, mac and cheese may be wonderful—your kids probably love it. Yet this food, like packaged breakfast cereal, should be part of a balanced diet that includes plenty of fresh fruits and vegetables, including fresh fruit juices (not sweetened drinks). To paraphrase the Scriptures (our apologies), "Man does not live by mac alone."

Single mothers are more likely to report that they do "actual cooking" for their children, perhaps because these women had primary responsibility for meals and other household chores during their marriages. Even so, busy single mothers often tell us they lose the desire to cook following a divorce. They buy and serve many more prepackaged, throw-it-in-the-microwave dinners.

■ ■ ■ ■

Let's face it: Convenience food is convenient! That's why so many of us—married, divorced, or single—favor convenience foods at the end of a busy day. Yet as you read and check the labels on many of these food items, you're sure to notice high amounts of fat, high amounts of calories, and high amounts of sodium. For most of us, so-called convenience foods are a convenient way to add pounds.

Here's a breath of fresh air: Among fast and convenient meals, pizza can actually be a healthy choice! As with cereal makers, pizza producers are finding their way to whole-grain flour. Even if you're a deep-dish fan, sample a thin-crust offering and see if you can make the switch. Thin-crust pizza has fewer calories and far fewer carbohydrate grams than are found in typical or stuffed-crust varieties.

If frozen pizza is a significant part of your diet, try getting more involved in the meal. Chop up some fresh vegetables and add them to the top of the pizza before baking or microwaving. Buy low-fat shredded cheeses and add these to the top of the packaged pizza before cooking. Involve the kids—sprinkling veggies and spreading cheese can be a fun family activity, building anticipation for the meal. If you're a sauce fan, consider buying inexpensive sauce and adding some to the top of a pre-packaged pizza. But a word of advice about all pizza sauces—watch the sodium level. It can be difficult to find a low-salt, healthy, tomato-based pizza sauce.

Used in moderation, fresh vegetables, low-fat cheese, and extra sauce need not add much cost to your meal. Frozen pizzas are frequently used as price leaders by grocery stores and major discount chains. Since you're saving money on the pizza, go ahead and buy that fresh green pepper, some leafy spinach, or a tomato. Buy low-fat cheese on sale and use it sparingly. If you can find a healthy sauce and your kids like it, add a half-can or partial jar to a large family-size pizza. Your kids will learn to love "improving" the pizza before it goes into the oven.

One of our "champion" single moms—she's raising four kids by herself—told us her kids loved burgers and fries, but she couldn't afford to take them out for fast food. She wasn't happy with the health consequences of her kids eating high-fat meat and high-carb potatoes so frequently. Her solution to this challenge may surprise you!

"I switched my kids to turkey burgers," Elana confides. "I thought they'd be upset with the change, but they hardly even noticed. Jon is old enough now to help with the grilling—he loves flipping the turkey burgers as they cook. Turkey is so much leaner than beef. There's a lot less splattering in the pan.

"I use a dark bun and low-fat cheese, and from there the kids build their own," she continues. "I keep lettuce, tomato, pickles, light mayo, and usually some jalapeño peppers around the house.

We all make burgers together—it's a family activity that becomes our family meal."

Even Elana's youngest child (a four-year-old girl) gets involved in choosing the toppings for her burger, always insisting "I can do it!" when Mom or a sibling tries to help. In search of healthy food options, Elana happened onto a family fun time that brings her kids together in the kitchen during the afternoon.

Instead of deep-fat fries, Elana bakes sliced potatoes in her oven, using a flat cookie sheet. She stays light on the salt and says she's experimenting with seasonings; so far the kids love the fries and don't realize their potatoes aren't really "fried" before serving.

"We aren't a tofu family," Elana laughs. "We do burgers and fries. So instead of fighting that, I decided to improve it. So far the kids love the turkey, and without the deep-fat frying, I'm fine with my kids eating potatoes—potatoes are very filling and very cheap."

If a busy mother of four can somehow find the time to grill and garnish burgers plus bake sliced potatoes (with the kids helping along the way), maybe her ideas might work in your household! Instead of microwaving every meal, relearn the joys of stove-top cooking and oven-baked treats. Along the way, look for healthy alternatives to the choices your kids already love.

Lifestyle and Fitness

Not surprisingly, many single moms report weight gains after divorce. "I started eating when Mark left me," one single mother told us. "That was 36 pounds ago, as of this morning."

We often insert this question in our single-parenting seminars: "How many of you exercise or work out on a regular basis?" In response, typically a few hands are raised. (We make no effort to determine what "on a regular basis" means.) Then we home in for the kill with our follow-up question: "How many of you live in condo communities or apartment complexes that have a fitness center or exercise room on the premises?" There's a lot of laughter as many hands go up—sometimes half the people in the room raise their hands.

The disconnect is the same across the country. Few single parents tell us they exercise regularly; quite a few admit they live in communities where a fitness center or workout room is literally just a few steps away.

Your children are learning about lifestyle and fitness principles by what you do, not by what you tell them. If your daily life screams "couch potato," you are likely to raise children who are overweight and not physically fit. If, however, you build exercise into your regular routines, your children are likely to model themselves after your behavior, learning healthy habits and good practices at an early age.

■ ■ ■ ■

It's never too early to begin teaching fitness. Many popular fitness centers that cater to women in their 20s and 30s include child-care facilities on the premises. Whether or not the children get a chance to work out, they definitely accompany Mom on her visit to the gym. Even in this way, experts assert, young children learn that Mom values physical fitness and staying in shape. As they become old enough to exercise, these children may want to join Mom in her workout sessions, particularly if the activity of Mom's choice involves aerobics, dancing, kick-boxing, or similarly upbeat moves.

One of the fastest-growing video-game segments at present is dance-based motion, usually involving a stepping pad that wires into your computer, tracking the dance moves of one or more participants while keeping score of the contestant's ability to dance correctly. Christian companies have noticed the trend: You can now purchase software and Christian music tracks that transform your television or computer monitor into a Christian version of these "dance fever" machines, combining physical fitness, helpful exercise, and contemporary Christian music into a fun activity for your own living room, kids' room, or den.

Can't afford a few tokens at the arcade, let alone the price of a new video game for your home? Exercise doesn't have to cost money.

Depressed, stay-at-home single moms often tend to gain weight as a direct consequence of snacking too much, eating the wrong foods, and failing to get enough exercise. If you don't live in a community with a fitness room, if you can't afford the membership fee of a workout club, get up off the sofa and take the kids for a walk. Got a pet? Get up and walk the dog; bring the kids along and make a daily walk part of your ongoing routine of physical exercise.

> The stress of a divorce may trigger a reversion to old habits, such as smoking and drinking, that are not healthy for the adult or for the children.

Getting up and moving around—with or without music—strengthens your cardiovascular system, speeds up your metabolism, and lowers your eventual risk of such diseases as adult-onset diabetes. Almost any level of physical activity can be helpful to your overall health: running the vacuum cleaner or climbing stairs to your second-floor condo are simple steps to better fitness.

Your children are likely to copy your choices. If you aren't active, they may not be. If you're a dancing, stair-climbing, rollerblading single mother, your kids are likely to grow up physically fit, healthy, and enjoying good exercise.

Single moms in cold climates often tell us that bad weather limits their ability to get outdoors. We respond by noting that shoveling snow is a great family activity that involves plenty of exercise! One single mom in northern Wisconsin keeps beach-type sand toys in a hallway closet. During the winter, the same toys that helped the kids dig sandcastles at the lake become snow-moving gear for her three school-age children. Her kids enjoy piling snow, ice, and slush into forts, structures, and sculptures.

A number of single parents find themselves returning to smoking after a divorce, even if they had long since abandoned the practice while married. The stress of a divorce may trigger a reversion to old habits, such as smoking and drinking, that are not healthy for the adult or for the children.

If you must smoke, by all means move outdoors when you light up, keeping cigarette smoke out of confined spaces and away from young infants and children of all ages. Airborne contaminants such as cigarette smoke are increasingly suspected in a variety of lung-related diseases including asthma. Links between smoking and lung cancer continue to be explored.

It's worth noting that if your children grow up watching you smoke, they're likely to emulate your personal example rather than listening to your sermons about the evils of tobacco. They're much more likely to watch what you actually do than to listen to what you perpetually preach. If you don't want to raise kids that are hooked on smoking, don't light up while they're growing up.

Modest amounts of red wine are increasingly linked to improvements in health among both men and women, yet the key appears to be limited intake. Moderate, occasional red-wine consumption may be connected with increased cardiovascular health and is a possible factor in reducing the incidence of some types of strokes.

Most other uses of alcohol impact health adversely in ways that offset any benefits or gains from drinking. Be aware that any alcohol kept in your home can be an alluring target for curious children or teens eager to experiment with the "buzz" of drinking. Once again, what and how you model about lifestyle, including alcohol consumption, will impact the choices and health of your children for years to come.

■ ■ ■ ■

Building and maintaining good health as a single parent is a function of getting enough rest, establishing constructive routines, and making wise choices in the areas of diet, nutrition, exercise, and lifestyle. While none of us are perfect, most of us can find room to make significant improvements in our eating habits, in the amount of exercise we get, and in our commitment to avoid obviously unhealthy activities such as smoking and drinking.

Learning to get enough rest involves paying attention to your rare but occasional opportunities for an afternoon nap or some quick downtime. Learning to get a quality night's sleep means discovering the virtue and value of bedtime routines and keeping your mind clear of anxious, worrisome thoughts as night approaches. Banish worry and focus your reflection on praise, gratitude, and counting your blessings.

Physical and emotional wellness is a function of making small but consistent choices in positive directions. Radical diets that completely change your eating habits may work for a short time; however, they are unlikely to become a part of your new routines for life. It may be wiser to focus on small, realistic changes that you can make toward better health—preferring stairs to elevators, parking a bit farther from stores and offices, getting outdoors each day to walk with your children or to walk a pet.

Since there are many sources of stress in your life that are not under your direct control, try taking control over your diet, exercise, and fitness. Establish healthy habits and effective routines that model good choices for your children. Keeping your immune system strong helps you ward off disease and infection; keeping yourself healthy means that your children receive care from a parent who is alert, focused, and capable.

Rather than preaching wise choices to your children and then modeling less effective choices in your real life, strive for consistency in how you live. Show your children what healthy choices look like in their daily dining, resting, and exercise habits. Over time, they'll learn a lot more from your example than from your advice.

PART TWO

Helping Your Kids Adjust to Trauma and Change—Learning to Nurture Your Children

Clifton was only eight when his parents divorced. Placed in the primary custody of his birth mom, he felt abandoned and alone as his father relocated to another state, forming a new family. Although his mother eventually remarried, Clifton closed himself off from making an emotional connection with his stepdad. Despite the stepfather's best efforts, Clifton remained distant and aloof, unwilling to bond or connect with the new male in the household.

Meanwhile, Clifton carried intense contempt for his absentee birth father well into his adult years. Only now, as a parent himself and a partner in nearly a decade of healthy marriage, is he beginning to realize just how deeply his inner self has been affected. With the help of a trained counselor, he is starting to process the core difficulties that trouble him as a result of his parents' divorce.

Clifton's experience is not unique. Many adult children of divorce report lingering personal and psychological issues as a direct result of the splintering of their family during childhood. Anger, bitterness, resentment, fear of rejection, fear of intimacy, inability to trust—these and other reactions may be set in motion by the departure of a parent and the breakup of the birth family.

The impact of divorce on children changes over time. Children who seem to be coping well within a fractured family may emerge into a troubled adolescence. Children who seem peaceful and calm on the surface may withdraw into an isolated world of their own emotions, hiding away their deepest wounds and worries, unable or unwilling to express their true thoughts.

Other children, though behaving badly in the days and weeks immediately following divorce or separation, may emerge into a relatively calmer period of academic studies, involvement in sports, or other distractions. Yet later, as they begin to form significant relationships and consider lifelong attachments, even these well-adjusted children of divorce may confront lingering doubts and fears.

Emerging studies confirm that children often carry these struggles and scars well into their adult years and into their subsequent experience of marriage and family. Previously well-adjusted children and teens may struggle to form key attachments as young adults, fearful of making or keeping commitments in a relationship. Some believe that if they let themselves love too deeply or attach too closely, they will only lose the one they love—a belief formed and informed by their own early experiences with marriage and family life.

A generation ago, social-service workers speculated that divorce did not have a major negative impact on issues of child development and mental health. Now that longer-term studies are emerging, this doubtful premise is revealed as wishful thinking. Reality is more complex than earlier generations had hoped. Divorce leaves scars in children and youth that may last throughout their lives.

We may be unable to control the duration or longevity of our marriage relationships, yet we are much more responsible for the way we explain reality to our families when our marriage comes to an end. Our children will be watching what we do and listening to what we say, processing what they see and hear, framing and exploring their own internal sense of right and wrong.

■ ■ ■ ■

How we nurture our children—in the immediate aftermath of separation and divorce, as well as along their continuing journey through life—will shape not only our children but also generations yet to come. If we can give our kids hope and confidence in the midst of trauma, and if the confidence we give them is rooted in a realistic view of human relationships and outcomes, our children may be less likely to repeat our mistakes. Instead, they will learn from our experiences in ways that are positive and instructive.

In the next four chapters we'll examine the ways in which you can nurture your children during and after a divorce, as the breakup of their birth family shatters their personal security and fragments their sense of permanence and stability. We'll discuss how to allow your kids the emotional space they may need to process difficult family issues in their own way and time.

We'll look at how the way in which you frame your own story and build your new family identity will help your kids apply the story to themselves and retell it for succeeding generations. In the process, you may need to rethink your own beliefs about the limitations and difficulties of the single-parent family.

We'll look at issues related to adjusting the behavior of your children, exploring together how a lone parent must and can retain control of her kids. We'll consider step-by-step methods of achieving meaningful results in managing and shaping the choices your children and teens may make.

Finally, because few other long-term parenting tools are as powerful as direct, open, loving communication, we'll explore together how to keep the lines of communication as open as humanly possible while your children grow and mature.

5

Appropriate Grieving

Allowing Your Children
to Mourn What They've Lost

■ ■ ■ ■

*The notion that children are resilient and
quickly recover from divorce is simply misleading.*

JUDITH WALLERSTEIN,
The Unexpected Legacy of Divorce

Children mourn the loss of their family unit in different ways as they move through the seasons of their lives. A child who appears to be coping very capably with separation issues may erupt later with unforeseen hostility, symptoms of withdrawal, or both. At the exact moment you may want to put your divorce behind you and move forward, your child may be coping anew and afresh with the pain and loss of a split family.

Effective parenting requires us to allow our children plenty of room for appropriate grieving. Their sense of loss is real—it is rooted in a substantive and lasting truth. Something they value has been taken from them, and they are unlikely to get it back. Something once whole is now broken; something permanent failed to last. Even a young child recognizes intuitively that the world is now different, and not in a way that the child perceives to be good or helpful.

■ ■ ■ ■

Time and again, younger children of divorce express a clear preference for both parents to remain in the same household, even if there is arguing, fighting, and open tension between the two adults. Children adjust to fighting and tension as normative within their family experience. While they almost certainly prefer a peaceful home to a stressful one, children continually prefer the security of a whole home, peaceful or not, rather than a broken household from which one parent is absent.

The departure of a parent, even if the child sensed or anticipated this departure, triggers fear at both rational and subrational levels. *What will happen to me,* the child wonders, *now that my parents are no longer living together? How will my life work out? Will I ever be "normal" again?*

Older children and teens are savvy enough to realize the probable financial impact of changes in their family system. *Will we be poor? Will I be unable to attend the university I hoped for? Is my hope of having my own car becoming an impossible dream? Will I have to get a job sooner than I thought?*

At deeper levels, children and teens worry about the loss of love: *If Dad is leaving us, does he really still love us? What happens if Mom quits loving us too? What will become of our family, of us children? Who will care for us if everyone we trust is suddenly missing from our lives?*

Mourning happens. The way in which you allow and permit appropriate grieving will show your child where the boundaries are in expressing emotions. The manner in which you react to your child's sense of loss and suffering will convey to your son or daughter the depth of your love for him, the intensity of your affection for her.

Infants and Young Children

The well-being of very young children can be directly linked to the amount of stability and normalcy within their daily environment. The degree to which a very young child mourns the loss of a parent will vary depending on the amount of daily, ongoing, routine contact with that parent that the child has experienced while the marriage relationship was intact.

Debbie's husband served in the armed forces. When her marriage ended, Debbie was left to raise a five-year-old son and a young daughter who had not yet experienced her first birthday. Not surprisingly, the divorce had very different effects on these two children.

Debbie's son had twice experienced his father's absences due to military service at sea. The active and inquisitive first-grader was

"It isn't fair," the son would say constantly... "Why can't I go live with my dad?"

excited about his dad's career, filling his room with photos of his dad in uniform. A tour of one of his father's duty ships was a highlight of his life. From that day forward, Debbie's son announced to everyone that he, too, would one day join the navy.

Before the divorce, during the times that his father was based at home, Debbie's son played with his dad most evenings. The two laughed together and had what Debbie describes as an "active, all-male" style of play—impromptu wrestling matches and other highly physical interactions. The natural result was a strong father–son emotional connection that could endure the occasional times of separation caused by active duty.

Debbie's daughter, born while her dad was at sea, had very little "face time" with her father. The marriage relationship was already in crisis by the time the young baby first saw her dad. Perhaps because he already knew that the marriage was ending, the otherwise loving father made little effort to pick up, hold, or cuddle his daughter, preferring instead to play with his son. Debbie now believes that this may have been a conscious decision on her ex-husband's part, an effort to shield himself from his own pain and loss as he ended the marriage.

In any event, the divorce was highly traumatic for Debbie's son, yet almost a nonevent for her infant daughter. The way in which the two children processed the absence of their dad was affected not only by their very different ages at the onset of the divorce, but also by their varied experiences with their parents.

Debbie's son reacted to the divorce with open anger and hostility, blaming his mother (who received primary physical custody) for the absence of his dad.

Having always felt loved by his father, the son was unable to process so many sudden changes—Dad was leaving permanently, Dad had a brand-new apartment, Dad's girlfriend was living with him in the new place, Dad's girlfriend was having a baby, Dad now had another son whom he perhaps loved more or better.

The issues were too complex for a young boy to understand. As the postdivorce environment unfolded around him, Debbie's son became angrier and angrier. Meanwhile, the daughter—who had little experience of an active, involved, on-site father figure—bonded closely with her mother and seemed to exhibit no particular trauma or stress without an adult male in the home.

Debbie's son was implacable at first: acting out by yelling and screaming, throwing tantrums, intentionally frightening his sister, and calling his mother as many bad names as he knew. As the outward signs of his anger subsided (six months to a year, by Debbie's report) the growing boy withdrew into grieving. Less absorbed now with hating his mother, the son began feeling sorry for himself for long periods of time, making his room into a shrine to his lost father.

"It isn't fair," the son would say constantly during this phase of his adjustment to a single-parent home. "Why can't I go live with my dad?"

Now school-age, he would withdraw to his room for hours at a time, playing with toy ships or lying on his bed staring at the ceiling. Instead of yelling at his mother, he withdrew from her presence, hiding himself away, professing not to be hungry at mealtimes. Debbie felt herself losing him.

Busy processing her own grief and loss as her marriage ended, Debbie was heartbroken to feel so rejected by her own son. As she tried to reach out to him with consolation and affirmation, it seemed as though her best efforts all failed.

"It was almost better when he yelled at me," is Debbie's analysis today. "At least then he was communicating! I knew what he was thinking; I knew how he felt because he kept telling me at high volume and with bad language.

"When he started withdrawing from me I got really worried. What was he capable of? Was he going to hurt himself, or maybe hurt others?"

A Loss Is a Loss, for Everyone

Debbie sought counseling, not so much for her own divorce-related grief but because she literally could not bear the sense of withdrawal and rejection that she experienced with her son. As she told the counselor on her first visit, Debbie was "afraid of losing him just like I lost my husband."

This fear was not grounded in a specific danger of a change in custody: Debbie's ex-husband preferred not having primary physical custody of the two children from his former marriage. He would go on to father several children with his new partner. He would continue his new pattern of remaining emotionally distant from the children of his first marriage.

Debbie's fear was that her son would mourn the loss of his dad in ways that were unhealthy or antisocial. At a deeper level, Debbie honestly admitted to fearing the loss of her son's affection and love.

"My kids are all I have left," Debbie remembers telling her counselor. "I'm not willing to risk losing either one of them."

The counselor trained Debbie to see the world through the eyes of a hurting, frightened, now six-year-old boy. Debbie's son felt abandoned and rejected by his father—a feeling he could not reconcile with his previous experience of a dad who had played with him, wrestled with him, and expressed verbally that he loved him.

The conflict between these two worldviews—"Dad loves me" versus "Dad is abandoning me"—was causing a high level of fear and anger in the son. The conflict was normal and natural, the counselor assured Debbie, and the son's reactions were also normal.

Debbie wasn't convinced, and she changed counselors.

The next therapist, after briefly interviewing the son and spending three intake sessions with Debbie, arrived at the same conclusions as the previous counselor: Debbie's son was mourning the loss of his father; to date this grieving was well within normal limits.

The new counselor advised Debbie to keep in close contact with teachers and school staff, with the parents of her son's few friends, and with anyone else who interacted with the family. The purpose of this monitoring was to notice if Debbie's son began engaging in self-destructive behaviors or became maladjusted socially, causing problems for those around him.

For the second time, Debbie was not satisfied. "I wanted a better answer than that," she says wistfully. "I wanted somebody to tell me what to do so that I would get my son back. Instead of that, everyone kept insisting that my son's reactions were normal."

However, Debbie declined to get a third opinion, followed instructions, and kept in close contact with her son's teacher, a school social worker, and several other parents. Within a year her son was much less sullen, much less withdrawn, and was on his way to becoming a caring older brother to his younger sibling. Allowed room to grieve in ways that did not harm himself or others, he moved forward.

Adolescents and Acting Out

When we interviewed remarried couples and blended families for our book *Happily Remarried*, we met a teen female whose response to the breakup of her parents' marriage took an unusual turn.

Each year on the anniversary of her parents' divorce the girl dressed completely in black, even wearing a black armband. She called the day "D-Day" ("D" for divorce) and conducted an annual day of mourning. Her mother, seeing the wardrobe and accessories, wondered if her daughter was "going Goth."

When the mother remarried, the new stepdad in the home followed a risky course of action. Learning of the girl's behavior, the stepdad prepared himself by also dressing in black on the anniversary date.

The caring stepdad said nothing to his new daughter, he simply showed up at the breakfast table dressed all in black. He went to work that way. He stayed dressed in black throughout the course of the entire day. He did not explain his choice. He did not warn his wife in advance about what he was doing.

Hearing about this strategy, we could imagine it backfiring in the worst possible ways. It seemed to us an unwise intrusion into the privacy and self-expression of an otherwise reasonably well-adjusted teen. However, as is often the case when working with families in transition, we ended up learning from this stepfather's wise behavior and advice. Somehow, this particular stepdad managed to reach the heart of a teen girl who was hurting, communicating his respect for her.

"I wanted to show her that I cared about her, that if she was hurting it affected me too," the stepdad says of his choice. "I didn't know how she would take it, but I knew how I meant it—it was like shaving your head when you have a friend going through chemotherapy and losing all her hair."

The stepdaughter noticed, but said nothing until late in the day. When her question finally came it was framed without much attitude, more in curiosity.

"Why did you wear black today?" the stepdaughter asked after dinner.

"It's D-Day," was the stepfather's response. "The day your parents got divorced." By using the phrase "your parents" the stepfather clearly identified himself as being in a separate category from the girl's birth parents. By dressing in black, his intention was to show that he identified with the pain and loss that his stepdaughter was still experiencing.

He was mourning for and with his new stepdaughter.

"I didn't know what to expect. I half expected her to be angry at me for stealing her way of expressing things," the stepfather shared. "What really happened was the last thing I ever expected—when I identified with her pain, she decided to open up and trust me with her feelings."

For the next six hours, the black-clad child of divorce and her equally black-clad new stepfather engaged in conversation that was deep, meaningful, and memorable. Both of them wept at times during the encounter. The eventual result was a strong bond between stepdad and stepdaughter that continues to this day.

"If she hadn't worn black, I don't know if I could have reached her," the stepfather admits. "She was showing us her grief, right where we could see it."

Signs and Markers

Debbie's son acted out at first by yelling and throwing tantrums: clear signs of his anger. Later, the same son began to withdraw—a possible indicator of depression, which is classically understood as "anger turned inward." As Debbie watched her son experience these two reactions, she wondered how to respond.

A teen daughter of divorce chose to wear black, a color long associated with mourning in many cultures.

Children of divorce frequently exhibit outward signs and markers of their inner emotional pain and turmoil. As single parents, our fear is that we won't recognize, won't understand, or won't react wisely to these clues when we see them—making the problems worse when we really want to be helping.

Here's a look at some of those signs and markers, helping you identify and address appropriate grief—and seek professional help when it's needed.

1. Is my child's behavior different since the divorce, or is this an ongoing symptom of issues that existed before? If your child screamed at you in the aisles of the grocery store while you were married, and you are unable to control her fits of screaming in grocery stores today as a single parent, these symptoms may not say anything at all about how your child is responding to your recent divorce. Since the behavior predates the current issues, divorce can't be blamed here.

Look for noticeable changes you can quantify and explain. Was your student a high achiever before the breakup, bringing home good grades from school? If this pattern changes and your child is no longer a top student, you may be identifying a sign of mourning that is worth exploring further. Yet if below-average grades are normative for your son or daughter, divorce can't be held responsible for the fact that he or she doesn't make the honor roll.

Has your talkative son become quiet? Has your shy daughter become aggressive and outwardly assertive? These changes may have nothing to do with the divorce, but if they are quantifiable and occurring at the same time that your family experiences separation or loss, these may be outer signs of inner issues.

Single parents, especially mothers, often have an intuitive sense that something is wrong with their children. Trust your instincts, but if you turn to a counselor for help you'll be asked for something more tangible. You'll be asked to describe what you have seen, heard, and observed: In what ways is your son or daughter behaving differently now than his or her past patterns? When did you notice these changes? Why do you think the changes may be related to the experience of separation or divorce? Your answers will help a counselor explore the dimensions of your child's grieving.

2. Is my child's behavior a distraction, danger, or problem for others, including those in my own family? Start within your family circle: Is your son picking on his younger siblings more than he did before? Has the pattern become more aggressive, more persistent, or more troubling to you? In a family system, each member is affected by the actions and choices of the others.

If you have more than one kid at home, does one child frequently upstage the others, demanding more of your attention and focus, relentlessly insisting on your attention by acting out? Are you unable to give adequate attention to your other kids because one child is constantly upset or angry?

Do teachers, social workers, friends, or relatives report antisocial behavior by your child? Is there a pattern of getting into fights before or during school, talking excessively during class, or picking on other children at church or in the neighborhood? Does your child exhibit anger toward others?

Without rushing to judgment (your child may or may not be an instigator of violence or fighting), pay attention to the warning signs that your daughter or son is making life difficult for peers, teachers, soccer coaches, or others. Receive information graciously: Rather than racing to defend your child's honor, listen carefully to what the

T-ball coach is telling you about your son's actions on the ball field and at team meetings.

3. Is my child a potential threat to herself? This is one of the greatest fears any parent faces, single or married. It is typical for many adolescents to withdraw into a quiet isolation that may indicate loss of hope, prolonged sadness or despair, or clinical depression. These issues are common to the process of coming of age; your divorce may not be a factor in what your teen experiences. Even so, you are wise to watch for signs that your child is perpetually "down."

Many teens are upset when they don't get their way—when they are denied permission to attend a certain party or stay out past a pre-arranged curfew. Most teens are saddened by the loss of a relationship—a recent breakup with a boyfriend or girlfriend is likely to trigger depressive symptoms. Understand the timing of what you notice. Is there a clear external trigger for your daughter's sadness, or is it an ongoing, increasingly normative attitude and temperament for her?

Though remaining wary of the current rush to medicate children and youth for any and all types of symptoms, be willing to consider the limited use of prescribed antidepressants if recommended by your doctor or counselor. Some youth respond very well to a limited regimen of chemical aid. Their body chemistry reverts to more normal patterns after a brief interlude of prescribed care.

Watching and Waiting—or Intervention?

As we'll discuss in the next chapters, the environment in your home will play a significant role in your child's ability to make the needed adjustments from having a two-parent family to living in a single-parent house. When you create an atmosphere of trust, respect, and open communication, you are building conditions under which each family member can mourn openly, recovering at his or her own pace.

As you learn to identify the signs and markers of mourning, your choice will be whether to allow or indulge your child's moods and symptoms, or whether to intervene and perhaps seek professional help. You should have no hesitation at all in seeking the services of a professional counselor when there are behaviors or indicators that concern you. Your child's school has many resources in place and available; your church may also be a source of qualified help.

It will be important, as we'll discuss in chapter 7, to learn how to adjust behaviors, particularly in younger children, that are disruptive of or disrespectful to the routines and practices of your household and family. If you allow sadness or mourning to become an excuse for outwardly antisocial and unhelpful behaviors, you are not helping your child, yourself, or the others in your family. Learn to identify, confront, and manage behaviors that are not acceptable regardless of your child's internal anxiety.

> Try to keep a clear, informed picture of how each of your children is adjusting to the challenging new reality of living in a one-parent home.

The case of the teen stepdaughter we discussed earlier in this chapter revealed a visible outward sign of mourning. In that case the teen behavior was harming no one—although her mother had unfounded fears of involvement with Goth ideas and style. The daughter's manner of dress was a personal statement, not an attack on a sibling, parent, or stepparent. Within reason, learn to be flexible and accepting of self-expression when it is not harmful to others and does not pose a clear danger to anyone. Give your child space to mourn her loss.

Some single parents tend to overreact, regarding every normal phase of childhood development as a new worry. Other single parents, busy making a living and coping with their own sense of loss and mourning, fail to notice important signals that a child may be struggling.

Be aware of your own tendencies in this regard. Are you the fussy, overprotective type who is easily upset? Or are you so self-involved that your children are raising themselves at times? Look past your own issues and try to keep a clear, informed picture of how each one of your children is adjusting to the challenging new reality of living in a one-parent home.

When a child is acting out in anger, explore the reasons while learning to manage the behavior. When your child withdraws, pay attention without insisting that your teen share "everything" with you on demand. Be assured that in two-parent families united by a strong marriage, struggles to discipline children are very normal experiences, as are times of estrangement from temperamental teens.

If they are not harming themselves or others, and if their behaviors are within norms and patterns that are acceptable to you, allow your children to mourn in their own ways. Some children arrange and rearrange their rooms almost endlessly, asserting control over the few things that seem to yield to their wishes. Some cling indefinitely to the hope that their parents will reunite, long after Dad has remarried or Mom has shown them the divorce papers.

■■■■

Simply stated, it isn't wrong when your children mourn—it's normal. Appropriate mourning can be a healthy release of the pent-up tensions that are part of family change. Get past your defense mechanisms and do not feel personally attacked each time your child wishes you and your ex were still together. Allow your young child to talk freely and naturally about their missing parent, expressing thoughts and feelings related to the breakup in their own way. And speak positively about your ex; try to be on your own best behavior.

Here's a theme that threads its way throughout this book: Express your love to your children generously and frequently. As much as possible, express to them also that they are loved by their other parent, the less visible one, the one who may have acted so very badly. It may seem difficult to defend your ex in this way, yet you are actually defending your child against a deeper and more difficult season of loss.

It is extremely important to the well-being of a young child to feel loved by both of the parents who brought her into the world. If she has experienced two parents and is coping with the loss of one from her daily world, reassure her that her absent parent loves her very much, despite living elsewhere.

As they mature, older children will form their own assessments about whether or not Dad continued to love them after he left your home and formed a new family. The conclusions they reach may differ from your own, but should not be shaped too intensely by your views. Keep an open mind and a positive attitude about whether your former partner does indeed love his or her children. Assume, if at all possible, that the missing parent still loves his or her kids.

Finally, understand that sadness is a part of life. Sit down with younger children and watch an animated movie such as *Toy Story 2* or *Cars*—these generally upbeat and well-told stories contain a surprising amount of sadness.

Sadness happens. When it is time for mourning, weep with those who weep, including the littlest ones in your household. Pay attention to their words and actions in case you need to adjust their behaviors or seek professional help. Yet within reasonable limits, allow each of your children to mourn and be sad.

The good news about loss is that it often encourages us to treasure more dearly the relationships we still have. In a bittersweet way, your relationship with your children may actually be improved by the suffering that you endure together. This shared experience of sadness and suffering can bond you together as a stronger, more caring, more tightly knit family circle.

Face your present challenges with clear-eyed honesty. View your potential future stresses with optimism and hope. Others have found their way through these dark and difficult valleys, and so can you.

The very fact that you are a single parent means that there is something in your life that is deeper than mourning: You still have children. Cherish these gifts from God while they are under your roof—you have been entrusted with greatness.

When the mourning ends, other seasons will follow. Until then, welcome and trust the ways your kids experience and express their emotions. Help them shape and view their own experiences in ways that are positive and redemptive. As we'll learn in the next chapter, a lot depends on how you tell your own story.

6

Telling Your Story

Shaping the Way Your Children
See Themselves and Others

■ ■ ■ ■

*I know that I loved my children
before the divorce—what surprises me is
how much more I love them now.*

LYNNE, SINGLE PARENT

We've been learning from divorced persons for more than two decades. Along the way, we've seen clear trends in the way divorce affects a person's thinking about his or her identity. Divorce sometimes does more than destroy a marriage. It goes on to diminish the self-worth and emotional balance of those who experience it.

Divorce can lead to a shattering loss of self-esteem in even the most confident of adult men and women. Divorce shatters our outward relationships but can equally erode our inner understanding of who we are. Over time, we begin to see ourselves as defined by the negatives we have experienced, rather than in terms of our other life pathways, our gifts and graces, and our potential.

A Downward Progression

There is a fairly typical progression that occurs in many persons, most particularly among women, in the aftermath of a divorce. It begins with this realization: "I am a person who has experienced a failed marriage."

This awareness—that one's personal journey has included failure in a key aspect of one's life—is rooted in fact. The trauma and difficulty inherent in the end of a marriage relationship are significant. It is not surprising that this area of extra sensitivity is writ large in our imagination and our sense of identity.

This understanding is not harmful in itself—in fact, embracing the facts of one's true journey is a health-giving exercise. However, the progression often continues beyond this acknowledgment of fact into deeper levels of self-doubt and self-recrimination. At these deeper levels, significant damage occurs to the identity and emotional wellness of the divorced and alone man or woman.

The second stage of this progression is, "I have failed in my marriage." Here the interpretation becomes more deeply personal. Now our statement is much more about our own culpability and our own limitations. Instead of admitting to being present at an unfortunate situation—for example, "I was in a train wreck last week"—now we are moving to another, deeper level of understanding. Rightly or wrongly, we are now saying something to the effect of "I caused a train wreck recently." Here we identify not only our participation in something we view as a failure, we also view ourselves as having caused, contributed to, or created the failure.

There may be some level of accuracy in this understanding. Which of us does not fall short? Many of us experience times of personal failure at some level during our primary relationships, including our marriages. More than a few of us finally begin to understand ourselves as we see ourselves through the lens of a close, intimate relationship such as a marriage union. Surrounded by such closeness, the images we have of ourselves and our identity are broken up. We are not as smart, not as capable, not as universally adaptable as we once believed.

Hence the awareness "I have failed in my marriage" may have some basis in the established facts of our divorce. Certainly it is significantly true for the partner who breaks his marriage vows, gets involved in an affair, then chooses to leave his wife for a new relationship. It is not inaccurate to attach the label "failure" to such openly negative behaviors and choices.

When we make a commitment and break it, when we violate a known and readily understood part of God's design for our life, it is true we have failed. When we allow chemical abuse or an addiction to pornography to undermine and spoil our relationship with our marriage partner, it is true we have failed. When we fail to control our anger, lashing out with verbal or physical violence against our partner or our children, it is true we have failed.

All of these highly visible external failures are markers indicating that we need to turn from our wrongful actions and seek new pathways. In biblical terms, this is known as repentance: renouncing evil, turning away from old patterns, and making a new start in ways that are redemptive and beneficial.

To identify that we have failed in these ways is a key step toward becoming new. To this extent, when we identify ourselves as having caused or created a failure, we establish a strong potential for changing our ways, and thus also for changing the reality we live in on a daily basis.

The road to real redemption is paved with markers identifying *ourselves,* not those around us, as persons who have been wrong and done wrong, children of God who need healing, restoration, and change. This is the road all of us travel, married and divorced, parents of intact families as well as single mothers and fathers struggling to raise their children alone.

Defining Ourselves

Yet in addition to serious wrongs, there are smaller ways to fail, ways that are much less visible and thus seemingly less important. These smaller failures are part of the human experience and do not usually cause the end of a marriage. Yet when a marriage does end, our awareness of these smaller failures, and our self-identification as a cause of or contributor to these failures, tends to move us to the second stage of the progression: "I have failed in my marriage."

At times the shame or guilt of these smaller failures is largely misplaced. We have been frail and fallible within the context of our marriage. So is every other human who gets married. The healthy marriages we see are unions of two frail persons who make mistakes, who fall short, who make unwise choices, and who often reveal themselves to be unwise persons, at least in some categories. There are no perfect persons—in the history of the universe only One has emerged.

Smaller failures define our human nature for what it is. We can learn from these smaller failures whether we remain married or whether we endure the end of a cherished relationship. Learning about ourselves is a positive outcome as we begin to confront our limitations, identify our blind spots, and recognize our weaknesses. Learning about our true character helps us to move in the direction of personal growth and maturity. It's a direction in which we all need to travel.

The problem, though, is that some of us who experience the end of a marriage begin to identify our small failures as overall indications of our personal worth. We see our own small failures and missteps as having primarily caused or essentially led to the divorce. We magnify the ways in which our normal imperfections inevitably led to our driving away our partner or failing to keep the marriage relationship intact and functioning.

For example, did you gain some weight while married? After a divorce, you may believe that your weight gain drove your partner away. You may blame yourself, identifying your lack of self-control as having caused your partner to run away with a more attractive co-worker or friend. The problem with this line of reasoning is simple to see: There are a lot of married men and women who have gained weight and yet remain in healthy, committed unions. Many people who continue to live on this planet continue to gain weight, particularly as they bear children, reach middle age, or become less physically active.

Yet in the mind of a divorced person, these lesser issues may loom as primary factors in the end of the relationship they treasured. From the first step—"I have experienced the failure of a marriage"—these persons often move as a matter of course to the next level of thinking: "I have failed in my marriage."

The Lowest Point

From there it is a smaller step to the third and most destructive phase of this progression: "I am a failure at marriage." Now we have made a powerful statement about our own identity, labeling ourselves in negative ways. Now we are not talking about what we did, but instead about who we are.

When we see ourselves as failures, we set powerful forces in motion that tend to bring about self-fulfilling prophecies. The greater the extent to which we see ourselves as being failures, the more likely we are to actually fail. We become what we believe ourselves to be. The reality we live in conforms more closely to what we expect, given our remarkably low self-image.

This chain of reasoning, from "I have experienced a failure" to "I have failed" to "I am a failure," moves persons through progressively lower levels of self-confidence, self-respect, optimism, and hope. A lingering sense of being an unworthy or unacceptable person becomes a constant companion of these troubled, postdivorce single parents.

An astonishing number of remarried persons, both men and women, bring this "I am a failure" mind-set into a new relationship. Having someone else find us attractive is a temporarily soothing balm that offsets our pain at being failures. Yet inwardly, our low self-esteem continually erodes our confidence, giving us more and more fears that our new marriage will end up just like the one before.

We counseled a man who was several years into his fourth marriage. As he shared about the three previous unions, we heard him label himself through all the phases of the progression we have just discussed. "I am a failure at marriage," the man eventually told us in a soft voice as we listened to him. Not surprisingly, his fourth marriage was in serious trouble—hence our involvement with him.

This man's behaviors within his second, third, and fourth marriages could not in any way be characterized as "major" failures. He had not been unfaithful. He had not been involved in substance abuse or domestic violence. Rather, his sagging levels of confidence and his low self-esteem caused him to live down to his very low impression of himself. Believing himself to be a failure, he eventually let himself think he had failed his current wife and his current family. Each time, the only option he could see was to end the relationship and move on because he had failed again.

We find this same perspective in some remarried women that we counsel. Although they remarry with high levels of optimism, these women's own internal sense of self-worth remains quite low. In the back of their minds, often below the level of conscious thought, they see themselves as failures, persons for whom a happy and fulfilling marriage is just not an option.

"I'm a failure at this whole marriage thing," one young woman told us. "I've tried it twice already—I just can't make it work. I don't know what's wrong with me!"

Her comments reveal the third and deepest level of the progression. Instead of saying "I have been in a marriage that failed"—a factual reality—she was telling us, "I am a failure." This is not a fact; this is a statement of her own personal opinion, which she is likely to keep living out for as long as she believes it to be true. By seeing herself as a failure, she is much more likely to experience the end of any future relationship. Her expectations set her up to fail. It would be a miracle if she succeeded in a new marriage in spite of this mind-set.

This particular woman shares that she has had two serious dating relationships since her second marriage ended. Neither of these relationships worked out well, the woman reveals. "I end up driving people away," she declares of herself.

It's How You See Yourself, Smarty

The amazing success of the "For Dummies" books reveals how many of us feel about our gifts, graces, and abilities. We are far more likely to self-identify as "dummies" than as "brilliant."

A book called *Microsoft PowerPoint for Brilliant Techno-Geeks* might sell a few copies—although the buyers probably wouldn't need to purchase it. Instead, what sells millions of copies is a book whose title announces that it is "For Dummies." We see the title and immediately think, *Aha, that's me!*

In the same way, postdivorce single parents often view themselves as incapable, lacking what they need to succeed. As we've discussed in this chapter, many of us allow the baggage of a failed relationship to become the defining factor in the identity we carry forward. Dragging this weight into a relationship limits our possibilities and reduces our chance to be happy and fulfilled. After all, we may reason, we don't deserve happiness and fulfillment—we are failures!

If it were only our own lives that we ruined, perhaps this calamity would be more acceptable. Yet reality is more challenging than this. When we think of ourselves as failures, it affects the way we interact with the world around us, including our children. Consciously or unconsciously, our sense of being a failure may transmit itself to our children and affect the way they view themselves. They may identify their own family experience as being part of a "train wreck" because their single mother or father believes this and behaves as if it is true.

> How you view yourself and your life experiences...to a large extent may determine the way your children think about their own lives and futures.

Your optimism or pessimism about your own identity, your beliefs about your prospects for the future, and your opinion of the dynamics of your family will be picked up by your children, even at a very young age. Many of them will mimic your view of reality, agreeing with you—whether you see the future as impossibly difficult or whether you believe a beautiful sunrise is just about to grace the near horizon.

How you view yourself and your life experiences will affect the way your children see you, and to a large extent may determine the way your children think about their own lives and futures. Your pessimism can have a deep, powerful, and contagiously negative effect on your children's mind-set and worldview. Your buoyant hope and enthusiasm can be profoundly energizing for children who have experienced trauma and loss.

It's how you see yourself, smarty!

With that in view, let's look at two hypothetical single mothers and how they might raise their families after a marriage ends. In both cases, let's decide that the husband left his wife and children, began or continued a relationship with someone else, and moved far enough away so that his children from the first marriage rarely see him and hardly know him as time goes by.

Each of our hypothetical moms is the partner who was left behind, abandoned by a husband and left alone to raise her children. Our two moms will start from the same place, yet they'll approach the future with two very different mind-sets, attitudes, and understandings of their personal identity.

A Vineyard of Sour Grapes: Mom #1

"It isn't fair," our first mom says as we sit down for a visit with her. "Look at all those other kids who get to grow up in two-parent homes, with a loving daddy who lives in the house. That's what my kids ought to be experiencing right now, but no—Jay had to go and run away with that bimbo! How can he do that to his own kids? How can he ruin their lives like that?"

Before we go further, let's unpack what this woman has just revealed. Let's begin with her last statement: Jay has "ruined" the lives of his children. This mother's words are directly defining the reality her children will now live in—their lives are "ruined" by their father's behavior and choices. This mother is giving a runaway ex-partner the ability to determine whether his children's future is bright and promising or negative and hopeless. She is telling her children that both their present and their future are now contaminated.

Who, exactly, is "ruining" the children at this moment?

It is not the absentee partner, for all his many faults. Instead, now it is the "I'm-just-a-victim" single mother, who sees her children's lives as ruined and their opportunities as limited because a biological father has chosen to walk away. Well, lots of biological fathers walk away from their families every day. Life shouldn't be that way, but it is! Somehow many ex-wives and children find the courage to move forward—becoming persons of talent, optimism, and great accomplishment. Far from being ruined, their lives and futures are defined by who they are as persons. They go on to high levels of achievement and create many positive family experiences later in life.

Let's take a further look at the belief system that is operating within this single mother's comments. For example, she explains to us that her ex-husband ran "away with that bimbo."

Can you imagine what her children are going to believe about their dad's new partner? Can you predict what they're saying about this woman right now?

"My dad ran off with a bimbo," Johnny, age nine, is telling the neighbor.

"I hate that bimbo!" six-year-old Sarah says about her new stepmom.

In the household in which they'll grow up, these two children will speak about their new stepmother, who has an actual name—Kaylie, we'll say—in ways that are deeply disrespectful. Children aged six and nine should not be taught to label any adults as bimbos. For one thing, it leads to obvious questions: What exactly is a bimbo? How does a person become one? Who fits in this category?

Our hypothetical single mom is doing serious damage to her children's ability to interact positively and successfully with adults, and specifically with the adults living in their birth father's home and new family. Once again, who is ruining these children now? It isn't their biological father, despite his bad judgment and his many faults. Instead, the person who is directly responsible for poisoning these kids' way of treating adults and the world around them is the mother we are now interviewing. She is the one teaching her children to call their stepmom a bimbo. She is the one showing them a way of demeaning other adults by introducing the concept of *bimbo* into the mind-set and vocabulary of two very young children. These children are hers to teach and train. She is accountable for how she does that.

■ ■ ■ ■

Let's unpack her statements a bit further.

Look at what this single mom's comments reveal to the children about their father. She has quite a lot to say. "How can he do that to his own kids?" the mother asks. Something bad has been done to other people. Who has done this bad thing? The birth father. Who has he done it to? His own children.

What has he done? He has "ruined their lives." So now it's not just that the kids' lives have been ruined, the statement reveals more: Their lives have been ruined, and Daddy did it! The reason these kids are living ruined lives is because their father did this to them. It is his fault that their lives are now ruined.

This statement also implies that a "loving daddy" lives in the same house with his children. This mother's words plant a powerful seed of doubt in her children's minds and hearts. Does Daddy really love me? If he did love me, he would stay in our own house. If he has moved out—which he has—then he must not love me.

Children of divorce are especially vulnerable to this line of reasoning. What child wouldn't feel unloved if her parent moved away? Fearing the absence or waning of their father's love is a normal reaction from these two children after their father's departure. Yet their mother is fanning the flames here by implying that "loving daddies" remain in the same house. Therefore, Daddy must not qualify as "loving" because he no longer lives here. Maybe he did love us, but he doesn't love us anymore. This magnifies the children's fears and plants injurious seeds of doubt within them. Afraid of losing their dad's love permanently, they may unconsciously withhold their affection for him. Alternatively, they may try far too hard to gain his love or approval.

Let's attempt to be fair here. It is at least possible that this father loves his children. Perhaps it's merely his ex-wife he's not so fond of. While we might want him to stay in his home and behave appropriately, his choice to leave does not guarantee us that he no longer loves his kids. Maybe he still loves them a lot! But now, seeds of doubt about that issue are being planted in his children's minds and hearts by an ex-partner whose negative outlook is having a powerful effect on two young and impressionable kids. Perhaps because she is insecure and self-critical, this mother is conditioning her children to wonder whether or not their daddy really loves them. She is playing on their fears, with the likely result of deepening those fears and hardening them into a mind-set.

■ ■ ■ ■

Then, she's doing at least one more thing.

"It isn't fair," is her opening statement. She quickly follows that first observation with "look at all the other kids." This mother is extending the coveted status of "victim" to her children. She is complaining that life is not fair—which it often isn't—then expressing her jealousy of other families.

Look at those kids over there—the ones in intact two-parent families—they are the lucky ones, this mom indicates. They have it made! While her own children suffer, she implies other children live in a bountiful and beautiful world inhabited by Ward and June Cleaver—two loving parents who share the same home and raise their lucky children with loving reinforcement.

This mother is training her children to resent and be jealous of others, and to especially resent and particularly be jealous of kids with two parents at home. This might be the natural tendency of a child of divorce anyway, but jealousy is not a trait that wise single parents choose to instill in their children's character. Wise single parents watch for signs of jealousy so that they can replace it with compassion, concern for others, and a balanced sense of sharing and being fair.

Wise single parents also realize that in today's world, blended families are quickly becoming normative in our society. As we mentioned earlier, as of late 2006, more than 1300 stepfamilies are formed each day in the United States. More than two million adults get divorced each year in this country, some of them for a second time or beyond. Social observers have widely reported that the stepfamily, or blended family, is "the family unit of the new millennium." And for at least the past decade or so, that characterization is statistically accurate.

Who, exactly, are the people this single mom's children are supposed to resent? With a more balanced look at today's reality, these kids would understand that many other children are growing up in a family circle that looks remarkably like theirs. Lots of other children live with only their mother or only their father. Many of their classmates at school live in blended families, formed after their birth parents got divorced and then married someone else. Many children live in homes with one birth parent and that parent's live-in, but not married, partner.

We've deliberately chosen a hypothetical parent so that we can take apart her statements as candidly as possible. With a real mom, we'd have sympathy, realizing that her worldview has been formed in the midst of difficult and damaging experiences. Our sympathy for the person would not change our views of her behavior, however: This mom is doing a lot of harmful things! As gently as possible, we would unpack this mom's beliefs about her life and her future, examining the potential harm she is doing to her children.

As it is, we can see what needs to change. This mother is raising children to believe they are victims. She is teaching her kids to be jealous of others, and to openly refer to their new stepmom as a bimbo. She is planting and reinforcing the belief that their dad has harmed them, and she's magnifying their natural fears that he may not love them anymore. She considers their lives to be ruined, and she tells them so! That's a lot of harm for one parent to cause. Notice again that this harm does not originate with the parent who walked away, but rather with the one who remained behind, poisoning her children's thinking.

A Bouquet of Colorful Possibilities: Mom #2

Now let's hear from our second hypothetical single mother. Remember, her experience has been exactly the same as the first woman's. Both of them have been abandoned by their husbands, left alone to raise their children.

We sit down with this second mother, ready to listen.

"This has been pretty rough," she begins. "I'm not over it, and I don't really know when or if I will be. I'm still not sleeping very well. Jennifer, my youngest, isn't sleeping very well either.

"There's a lot I don't understand, and a lot I don't know. But I'll tell you what I do know—we're going to get through this. I love my kids. They are bright and beautiful children. We're going to stick together, we're going to be a good family, and we're going to get through this.

"I will do everything I can to be sure my kids know they're loved and respected. Whatever it takes, whatever I have to do, that's how it's going to be. We're going to be a loving family, and we're going to have good times together!

"Already we're laughing at some of the movies the kids liked before all this happened. I can't tell you how great it is to hear these two kids laughing! They need some humor in their lives, after all they've been through. They need to laugh; they need to let out some tension."

■ ■ ■ ■

Listen to the voice of single mom number two. No—she isn't some perky, overcaffeinated morning-talk-show host. She's not a Pollyanna who sees everything through rose-colored glasses. She isn't living in denial; she isn't pretending that no one hurts. Listen to her—she's telling you the truth. She is telling herself the truth. And she is telling her kids the truth.

What is the truth?

"This has been pretty rough," the divorcee's statement begins. There it is, right out in the open. This experience of a marriage ending has been difficult. It's been hard for everyone. It isn't easy; nothing about it is simple. Yet for all its candor this statement doesn't blame someone, point fingers, or seek the label of a pitied victim. Instead, this is an eyes-open, matter-of-fact look at reality.

Reality continues.

"I'm not over it, and I don't know when I will be." Once again, a statement of life as it is. *I'm not over it.* This mom is not saying, "I ought to be over it by now," or "I am taking too long to recover." She simply states what can be established as fact—*I'm not over it yet.* She goes on to admit she doesn't know when she will be. In other words, she is not putting herself under some kind of expectation to be "healed" or "different" or "over it" within a certain period of time or by an established deadline.

Newly divorced single parents often place themselves under an unrealistic expectation that they should feel better, perform better, or "get back to normal" swiftly. Friends and relatives are often quick to dispense this same sage advice. Yet despite unhelpful family members and unrealistic expectations, this mom holds firm. She realizes that each divorced person's experience will be different—yet in general it takes time before normalcy returns. Even then you can be certain you'll experience a new normal—your old life is gone.

This mom wisely understands her own process. She isn't over it, and it's not possible for her, at this stage, to discern when she might be over it. She goes on to list some of the symptoms: She isn't sleeping well, and her daughter isn't sleeping well either.

Once again, this is a descriptive statement about life as it really is. This mom is not blaming the ex-husband for her sleep patterns, nor is she telling her daughter that the daughter's lack of sleep can be traced to an absentee father. Rather, she's being open and candid about how things are—it's been a while since the divorce, but two of us in this household still aren't sleeping well.

If your initial reaction to this mom's statement was to roll your eyes—she was way too perky or optimistic—then you weren't listening. If you had listened more carefully, you would have heard that this mom is still suffering, and that a return to normalcy has not yet happened for her. Her life is a work in process. Meanwhile, she isn't sleeping well.

■ ■ ■ ■

It is only after this candor has been established that this mom begins to unfold for us her philosophy about the future. "There's a lot I don't understand, and there's a lot I don't know," she tells us, admitting what is obvious. "But I'll tell you one thing I do know."

Now she has our attention. She's been honest and transparent.

She admits to her struggles. She admits she doesn't have her life figured out. But she's about to tell us one thing she knows. What is it?

"We're going to get through this," she asserts. Now she is telling life how it is going to be: Regardless of what it throws at her and at her children, they're going to survive and keep going forward. *Yes, life is tough, but we're going to get through this.*

"We're going to stick together, we're going to be a good family, and we're going to get through this." This is woman—hear her roar! This woman and her children are a family now.

> This attitude lays a foundation for success that is powerful and highly contagious.

What kind of family will they be? A good one! Not a defective one, not a collection of wounded victims, not a group of people who want to be pitied by others because of their miserable and ruined life.

No, this family is going to be a *good* family! They're going to stick together, face life with honesty and courage, and get through it. You can almost feel the surge of positive energy this woman is creating. *Obstacles, you'd better watch out—my family and I are going to get through you!*

This attitude lays a foundation for success that is powerful and highly contagious. What are these children going to believe about their family? They are going to realize their mom considers it to be a good family. Why shouldn't she see it this way? Won't this family be a loving place, a place where people care for each other and help each other, showing affection and kindness to each other? Isn't this family planning to stay together? Of course it is—this is a good family. It is highly likely that these children, no matter what they have experienced, will emerge from the whole process believing that today they live in a good family. They'll be right about that.

Now the second mother gets to some of the best parts of her statement.

"I love my kids: They are bright and beautiful children." Just listen to this mom's declaration of truth. Her children are bright and beautiful! They are not ruined victims, lacking the many advantages of other kids around them. They are not people who are deprived of opportunities or missing out on the good life. What are they? They are bright and beautiful children.

She goes on: "I will do everything I can to make sure my kids know they are loved and respected." She is taking personal responsibility here. She is not assigning duty or transferring blame to the absentee father. Rather, as the head of this household and the leader of this new family, she is declaring how things are going to be: She will do everything she can.

Toward what goal? Toward the goal of raising children who know for certain that they are loved and respected. If she can do this, her economic status will not greatly matter. If she can do this, it will not be highly important whether her children are accepted to Ivy League universities or get full-ride scholarships. This mother will be giving her children a priceless gift—the gift of knowing they are loved and respected.

Do you see what can happen when a partner runs away? Someone steps up to the plate and says, "I will do everything I can to make sure my kids know they are loved and respected." This is an awesome statement of personal responsibility and motivated leadership. You are hearing from an award-winning single mother.

What will the future be like for her family?

This mother's statement makes a declaration about this issue also. "We're going to be a loving family, and we're going to have good times together!" The kids are listening, and this is what they hear—their future includes being a cherished member of a loving family. There is safety and reassurance in this powerful message. It reaches to the core of a threatened, ruffled, uncertain child of divorce who is wondering about a lot of things, including the future. Now this child learns about the future from his or her mother: *As we go forward, we are going to be a loving family.*

It gets better. "We're going to have good times!" This could sound like false bravado or wishful thinking. It could sound like full-bore denial of the many difficulties of life in a single-parent family. It is none of that. Remember, you've heard what this mom is going through. You've heard that she isn't over it. You've heard that she isn't sleeping well and her daughter isn't sleeping well either. She was up-front and candid about admitting these things. She knows her struggles more fully than you do! She's already told you that life hurts.

But guess what? This mom says her family is going to have good times! What a powerful and energizing statement about their future. And all of us get a preview of that future as we see the family sit down together to watch funny videos. They used to laugh at these movies, and they still do. The movies are still funny; the things that made the kids laugh before the divorce have not lost their humor or their charm. This group can sit down together as a family, pop some popcorn, pour some store-label cola into plastic cups, and watch a movie.

■ ■ ■ ■

Almost—though it's absurd of course—you almost want someone to run away so this kind of family can emerge. Of course that's ridiculous, but notice how your paradigm has shifted. Instead of feeling sorry for this poor, suffering, deprived family—now you wish you lived in it!

Children make exactly these same connections. When their custodial parent tells them they are bright and beautiful, what do they begin to believe? When their custodial parent says she'll do everything she can to make sure these kids know they are loved and respected, how do these kids feel?

When a busy single mother says the family is going to stick together, that it will be a loving family, and that the family will have good times together, what does this tell a confused and frightened child about his or her future? The message sends all the right signals: The future is safe, the future is about being together, the future means being loved, and the future includes having good times.

That's the kind of future to think about if you're growing up in any family. It's an especially great future to consider if you're raised by a single parent.

Finally, this mom understands human nature quite well. Her kids need to laugh, and she knows it. She may not feel like becoming the family comic, but she knows where to find one—at the video store or the public library. She finds things that make her kids laugh, she slides the DVD into the machine, and she sits with her children and experiences with them the healing power of laughter. As the old cliché explains, laughter may just be the best medicine.

Faced with a difficult life, this mom admits it's tough, admits she doesn't understand it, admits there's much she doesn't know. Then she stands up tall and strong, regardless of her height and size, and tells the world how things are going to be—she is going to raise bright and beautiful children in a loving family that sticks together and has good times.

Let the future begin!

■ ■ ■ ■

As these two cases dramatically show us, our children's sense of well-being and worth heavily depend on how we see our life and how we speak about it. When we understand our situation as being difficult yet approach it with hope, we help our children have the same attitude and response. If we degenerate into misery and despair, blaming others and feeling sorry for ourselves, we may find that we live in a house where everyone else feels the same way.

As for you—what kind of house will you live in?

7

Raising Children Means Learning

How to Manage and Change Their Behavior

■ ■ ■ ■

*Single parenting is twice the work
with half the reward.*

MARTIN AUTENSMITH

Ask any mother of small children: Parenting is hard work.

From your perspective as a single father or mother, it may appear to you that two-parent families have it easy in the raising of children. Quite frankly, this is not even remotely true. Learning to parent effectively is always difficult, and intact two-parent families are challenged as both adults struggle to learn how to manage, adjust, and control the behavior of their kids.

Want proof of this? Spend a weekend at a large department or discount stores scanning for well-behaved kids. The results may shock you. You'll observe plenty of begging, screaming, tantrums, and fits. You'll see wild, unruly, and out-of-control children everywhere you look. Many of these kids will be from two-parent families.

Surprised? We'll go a step further. Some of the best parenting we see done today is happening in single-parent homes. Why? The answer is simple—with only one parent on duty, it isn't possible to transfer "problem kids" to someone else's care and management. A father can't busy himself at work, trusting his wife to learn how to control their children. A mom can't allow havoc all day around the house, trusting that when her husband gets home he'll be able to make the kids pay attention and mind their manners. There isn't an extra adult—in a single-parent home, there's no one else around to whom you can delegate your difficulties.

In two-parent homes, each parent often wishes that the other partner would somehow be magically transformed into a tough disciplinarian, an effective leader, or a superb household manager. The wife may see it as her husband's role, since after all he's the "head of the house." The husband may see it as his wife's chore, since after all "she's the mother around here." Two-parent households are often places where each parent loves to delegate the tough stuff to the other. The result is that the difficult tasks of parenting may be avoided or postponed indefinitely. The fruit of such avoidance is children whose behavior is out of control, children who never learn proper respect for adults and authority.

Two-parent households, although they may sometimes seem ideal to you as you struggle to manage kids without a partner at your side, do not have an automatic inside track to better parenting. On the contrary, with only one parent in the house, guess who has to learn how to manage the children effectively?

You're right—it's you.

■ ■ ■ ■

The good news is that even if it appears too late to get started, it's never too late to begin modifying your children's behavior, teaching them to respect you and to observe the boundaries, policies, and practices that you choose to establish. Your kids may be out of control today, but there is every reason to believe that in a few weeks or a few months, their behavior will be radically different.

The place to start is identifying your primary responsibility as the parent. As the adult in the home, your role is to set appropriate boundaries, check to be sure those boundaries are being kept, and then enforce the boundaries when a child tests your resolve or rebels against your authority. Kids will be kids. You can expect your children to test, explore, and challenge you at every opportunity.

When a single parent fails to set appropriate boundaries for the family, children tend to become more and more confused, angry, upset, and rebellious. This struggle may begin at an early age, but it will magnify as an unmanaged child navigates the treacherous waters of adolescence. Teens without boundaries keep testing the limits, taking ever more daring risks, hoping to eventually find a parent who cares enough to draw lines, build fences, and enforce rules.

The Five Hallmarks of Effective Single Parenting

You may be fortunate enough to be raising well-behaved children. If so, use the following section to reinforce what you've learned about doing effective behavior management for children and youth.

If you are already parenting young children or teens that seem to be out of control, don't worry that you've already lost the ability to manage their behavior. Instead, sit down with this chapter and discover your primary responsibility as the adult in the home. Start where you are, and begin to apply these lessons in small ways. The fruit of your work—and it will take work on your part—will be positive changes in the way your children and teens relate to you as a parent.

Setting Boundaries

Your very first task as a single parent is to *set boundaries* for your children. This means deciding what kind of language, personal cleanliness, tasks or chores, and other behaviors you are going to require in your own home. Instead of compromising and settling for chaos, think about how you'd like your house to function.

You may be living with your parents for a while after a divorce, thus reasoning that you don't really have a home of your own. Yet you do: Your children are yours. Wherever you are living, regardless of how many people are under your roof or who owns the property, you are the parent of your children. You are the one who has the duty, the responsibility, and the privilege of deciding what kind of boundaries will exist within your family. Boundaries are not about who owns the space; they are about how to manage your children's conduct.

Think about how you want your kids to behave. Be realistic, but realize that you do not have to settle for family conditions that upset or discourage you. Aim higher! What kind of children would you like to live with? What kind of household would you like to come home to after a long day at work or at school?

Set the boundaries as clearly as you possibly can, in ways that are age-appropriate for each child. Have your children repeat back to you what you are telling them, so you can be certain that they understand what you are saying. Listen carefully during this process: Do your children realize what you are now going to require? Do they understand the words you are using?

Do you want their rooms to be neat and tidy? If so, exactly how neat and how often? What precisely do you mean by a tidy room? Be extremely clear in what you mean. If you want everything off the floor in your teenager's bedroom (have you ever seen the floor in there?) then state clearly that "neat" and "tidy" mean that nothing is lying on the floor anywhere in sight. Explain the function and role of closets, dressers, clothes hampers, and hangers.

Do you want your three-year-old son to put all his toys back in the toy box, or perhaps the closet, at the end of the day? State this rule clearly and simply. Show him where the toy box is; escort him over to the closet. Add an evening ritual during which you inspect the room, searching for toys that are out of place. Explain clearly that, no matter how messy the room is during the day, when it's time for bed each item must be back in the toy chest or stored in the closet.

Do you want your teen son's homework completed before other activities, such as Game Boy, can begin? If so, explain this to him, using small words if necessary. Make sure his earphones are unplugged. Also, be sure that you physically have custody of the Game Boy(s) so that after you inspect all the homework to be sure it's complete, you can distribute the game cartridge or the control module to your son, who has now earned some playtime.

Do you want your kids' clothes to be cared for so they last longer and look nicer for longer periods of time? Be sure that you're age-appropriate (young children are not usually neat freaks, although the few exceptions are interesting to raise). If you want certain clothes hung up on hangers, say so, pointing the way to hangers and where they should hang.

If you want your teen daughter to return the sweaters or sweatshirts that she borrows from you, let her know when and how often. For example, specify that every item of your clothing must be returned to you each Saturday afternoon. Even if the cycle of borrowing begins again immediately, you will be setting a boundary and teaching a principle—clothes get returned to their rightful owner. This may have the added benefit of helping your daughter return clothes to her friends—let's face it, most of what she wears is borrowed anyway!

> As an adult in the home, you are carryng out your responsibility and setting up some rules that you expect to be obeyed.

Do you want each of your children to help with certain chores around the house? If so, do you want those chores performed at a regular time during the day or the week, or do you simply want them completed within a specific deadline? Once again, be simple, direct, and clear. Think about your home and family, then set boundaries that you are comfortable with. Explain those boundaries with simplicity and clarity, having your children repeat them back to you.

If your children seem out of control, don't try to immediately set a dozen new boundaries for them. You'll wear yourself out, and you probably won't succeed in making the needed changes. Instead, if you think of yourself as already running behind in the race to manage your children, start with small steps in the direction you'd like to go. Begin with one or two boundaries, perhaps with words you don't want said in your home or with one specific chore that you'd like for your teen son to accomplish each and every week.

Start with a few rules, but be clear: You are not making "suggestions" here. You are not opening the floor for a debate about how the household will function. Instead, as the adult in the home, you are carrying out your responsibility and setting up some rules that you expect to be observed.

Monitoring the Boundaries

Your next task as an effective single parent is to *monitor the boundaries* and to notice, in a timely and immediate way, whether your rules are now being carefully followed. If one of your children is ignoring or rebelling against the rules you have explained and reviewed, it's important that you pay attention and observe the infraction. Having effective boundaries means regularly monitoring your children to be sure that the boundaries are being observed.

For example, if you have a rule that all homework must be done before your son can go online and use his computer, it's not adequate to pass by your son's room, pause in the doorway, and ask your son if his homework is done.

"Yes, Mom!" he may say, whether the statement is true or not. Your son is not the one who monitors the boundaries—you are. Inspect, check, investigate, and confirm that your rules are being followed. It's not your son's job—it's yours.

About your children and homework: Look at it with them. Go over his reading with him. Review the math assignment with her. Sit down and scan the worksheets, look at the exercises, and check for the completion of whatever the teacher assigned. The more you do this, the more you are teaching your kids that not only are there boundaries in your home; these boundaries are actually being monitored by a parent who cares about compliance. If this is a change from your past behavior, you will need to be consistent and clear as you make the transition from being lax about rules and values, to being clear and serious about them.

There is absolutely no point in having boundaries and rules unless those rules and boundaries are backed up by timely and consistent monitoring. A rule that isn't enforced is nothing more than a polite suggestion from that quaint old mom or dad rattling around the house. If your children nod at you politely and mumble their agreement yet don't actually follow your rules, you are teaching them to disrespect you as an adult and as a parent. You will begin gaining their respect when you start to check their compliance—when you monitor the boundaries that you have clearly stated and carefully explained.

Do you want everyone's room to be clean once a week, at a certain time? If so, it's likely that most or all of your children will quickly clean their rooms about ten minutes before the deadline occurs. Since that is human nature, it may be helpful if you begin a habit of inspecting your children's rooms about one hour (depending on the child's age) before the deadline that you've set. Your purpose is to serve as a visual and verbal reminder that a deadline is approaching, and that you are absolutely serious about that deadline. You know what time it is!

Here is how your pre-inspection tour might sound:

"Oh my goodness, Caleb, look what time it is! It's already three o'clock on Saturday afternoon! That means Mommy will be coming back in just one hour, when it becomes four o'clock, to inspect your room. Look what still needs to be done! I see clothes on the floor, toys all over your bed, and a big mess by the door! You've got one hour to get this room looking sharp, buddy!"

You can expect Caleb to shrug his shoulders, perhaps saying something like "Awww...Mom!" or "I know, Mom!" in reply. But regardless of the response you may receive, you are sending your son a very clear signal. His room is being inspected right now—you notice and state that it doesn't pass inspection—and there's just one hour until the deadline, at which time the room better be ready.

When you come back in an hour, the hard work has already been done. You've already mentioned the rule, reinforced the rule, and pre-inspected the room with comments about where compliance is needed. Now, all that's left is to show up at four o'clock and discover that he's actually cleaned his room!

Your pre-inspection tour has just greatly increased the odds that Caleb will meet the deadline, clean his room, and thus show his respect for you as his parent. Single parents do not have the luxury of being sloppy or careless as they raise their children; there's too much at stake. Instead, single parents have the blessing and the privilege of learning how to manage, adjust, and control the behavior of their children. It should be one of your highest priorities as a mom or dad.

As you learn to state boundaries clearly, as you check to be sure that your boundaries are being observed, your children will learn something that is vitally important for their personal maturity. They'll learn that you say what you mean, and that you mean what you say. It's one of the most important lessons they can learn from an adult—about what it means to become and be an adult.

When you say what you mean and mean what you say, you are showing your children integrity in action. You are an example of consistency and virtue. No matter what else your children may witness in the world, by looking at your life they will now observe a person of integrity, honor, and commitment.

Now that you have set some boundaries and are beginning to monitor them, you are ready to move to the next level when needed. You can be certain of this: The next level will be essentially needed, probably sooner rather than later.

Enforcing the Boundaries

The next level—the third hallmark of effective single parenting—involves learning how to *enforce the boundaries* that you set.

Many single parents have at least one compliant child (often a firstborn) for whom it's often sufficient to simply explain what the boundaries are and then monitor them. Compliant children love it when you notice they are complying. They are energized by having a parent in the home that rewards their good behavior by paying attention, complimenting their obedience, or praising their character. It is sometimes possible to adjust the behavior of a compliant child by merely using a stern look, a timely word, or a simple comment.

If you're a single mom or dad with more than one child, it's unlikely that every one of your kids is highly compliant. Variety happens!

For less compliant (that is, more "normal") children, the task of enforcement will not only be necessary, it will become a regular feature of your parenting time.

Learn how to carry out strong enforcement: You'll be doing a lot of it.

However, the good news is this—the clearer, the more consistent, and the more determined you are, the more effectively you will shape and mold your children's understanding of what is expected of them. When your boundaries don't change, when your monitoring doesn't let up, and when your enforcement keeps on happening—children begin to learn. Their learning curve improves immensely when your boundaries are clearly set, monitored, and enforced.

Approaches to appropriate enforcement vary with the opinions of the parent, the age of the child, and the general temperament and character of the child that you are raising. Many parents report having at least one younger child for whom enforcement is as simple as "making a mean face" or being stern and gruff during a verbal rebuke. Particularly with younger children, it is sometimes adequate to enforce a rule by clearly indicating that you are displeased, upset, and not satisfied. When doing so, some parents report, they begin to get compliance from their previously uncooperative little one.

Parents of two- and three-year olds often discover that mean faces are not quite enough to produce the desired results. Be prepared to go further, having thought out for yourself how you will approach child discipline. Are you willing to smartly slap the hand or arm of an errant child? Decide this before you need to actually do it. Do you believe that appropriate spanking can be a form of showing your child that you love him or her? If so, make this decision prior to the time that a spanking may be indicated by your child's behavior.

Think through the issues involved in child discipline and decide for yourself how you will handle it when rules are broken. Communicate those consequences to your children in clear ways. Once again it is vitally important to mean something if you say it. Once you've said it, it is vital to follow through and impose the consequences that were discussed and described. Most children ignore a mother who always makes threats, but never carries them out! Most children notice if Dad talks tough, but never does anything about it. When your behavior teaches lessons like this, you can expect your children to be out of control.

Determining consequences. If you try to control your children without physical consequences, by using your strong emotional tone or your sharp words, be prepared to have your son or daughter attempt to charm you out of your perceived bad mood—rather than complying with the rule or staying within the boundary that you've set. This is why a consequence that seems limited to emotion or words may not be effective with many children. Emotions and words come and go; children learn to use these same weapons against you.

Children learn at an early age how to manipulate parents emotionally by withholding or expressing affection. Single parents, who may already be somewhat emotionally needy, are especially vulnerable to this kind of blackmail by children who simply don't want to behave.

Useful consequences, adjusted in age-appropriate ways, include the withdrawal or withholding of privileges or rewards. If the chores are not completed by the assigned time, then the weekly allowance will not be given. Should the room not be clean by the assigned deadline, then there will be no TV or computer time for the rest of the evening—not even if the room suddenly becomes a priority and the grumpy teenager suddenly begins cleaning it. The penalty should be announced in advance, then imposed without any hope of avoiding it if the rule is broken or ignored.

A teen who learns that he can avoid enforcement by completing his tasks *after* the deadline...has just moved the deadline. Whether he knows it or not, this growing son has just lost a measure of respect for you as a parent.

Although you stated a boundary, and although you monitored it, you broke down at the point of the enforcement. Your child—even at a very young age—will recognize this for what it is: a sign of weakness or indecision on your part. You can expect almost every child, and especially older children and teens, to immediately exploit any weakness or indecision that you reveal.

Weak, indecisive single parents produce children who believe that the world revolves around them, adjusts automatically to them, and changes its rules based on their own behavior or opinions. Consistent, effective single parents produce children who understand the concept of rules, limits, consequences, and good behavior. If you were trapped on a desert island with children in one of these two categories, which category would you choose? Most of us love to be around well-behaved children; we're just not sure that ours can turn out that way!

Single parents often use the trauma of separation and divorce as an excuse for their children's bad behavior. This fools no one: A rule is a rule. Separation and divorce can and do lead to sadness and difficulty. Yet it is not acceptable for a teen son who is angry about his father's departure from the home to respond by abusing his mother verbally or by constantly rebelling against her authority.

No amount of being abandoned makes this behavior suddenly okay or acceptable. It is not acceptable: It is a clear sign of disrespect. Your task as a single parent is to communicate clearly to your children what behaviors are okay in your household and in your presence, and what behaviors cross the line and must be changed or eliminated—or else consequences will ensue.

Negotiation. Some single parents naturally raise questions about negotiating with their children. If you are a highly verbal single mom who enjoys the give-and-take of negotiating each rule and boundary with your child, go ahead and enjoy yourself. However, it's always best to negotiate during the first step—establishing the boundaries—rather than at later steps such as monitoring or enforcing.

When you're ready to enforce a rule that has been clearly stated and consistently monitored, it's not the time to begin negotiations about whether or not there will be consequences, or what the consequences will be. Simply stated, it's too late for that! Your children should know that negotiation at the point of enforcement is a doomed idea. It won't work—not the first time, or the second time, or the time after that. At the point of enforcement, it's too late to try and talk a busy dad into a weaker, watered-down rule or consequence. When an effective mom notices bad behavior, she imposes consequences clearly and firmly.

In general, we do not recommend negotiation as an effective strategy for single parents. Having said that, if you want to raise a brilliant lawyer or judge, or perhaps the next president of the United States, go ahead and bargain with your child about every rule and every boundary. Maybe your child will grow up to become a skilled diplomat, a federal mediator, or a member of Congress.

Otherwise, shun negotiation in favor of boundaries that are clear and rules that are simple to understand. Be your own arbiter of "fairness"—chances are it's not a coincidence that you're the adult in the household! With clearly understood boundaries in place, get out there and monitor compliance—and make sure your kids see you doing the monitoring. Turn a polite but deaf ear to your children's excuses: Once you've made the rules clear, it's their job to comply, not argue.

The difficult task of enforcement is made immeasurably easier when you have clearly and consistently followed the two prior steps of communicating the rules and monitoring the boundaries. With some children, it will be enough to merely communicate and monitor. With most children, you'll need to complete all three steps: communicate, monitor, and enforce. But every time you enforce, you'll be making your role as parent simpler and easier in the future. Every time it becomes clear that you mean what you say, you are building a foundation for a future in which you say less, but achieve more by saying it.

Repetition

This cycle of setting boundaries, monitoring compliance, and enforcing consequences when necessary leads to the fourth hallmark of highly effective single parenting: *repetition*.

Most children, and in fact many of us who are adults, learn by repetition. How do you master a new skill on the computer, or a new software program that you have just downloaded, purchased, or installed? Long ago you might have read a printed instruction manual, back when those existed. These days, you'll learn by actually using the program—by repeating the tasks that you use the program to perform on a regular basis.

The more times you open a file in Microsoft Publisher, the better you'll understand how to use the program. The more times you upload a digital photo from your camera to a Web-based album site, the faster you'll get at completing the steps. Just like your children, you also tend to learn by repetition.

Most of us learn by hearing and seeing, then hearing and seeing again.

Your children learn in the same way. As you repeat your boundaries, as you monitor the rules to be sure that they're followed, when you enforce some age-appropriate consequences if those rules are broken, you are creating a cycle that teaches your children what is expected of them. At a deep psychological level this cycle is comforting and reassuring to your children. It helps them understand their correct place in the family system and in the household.

> When you firmly stick to your rules and make sure they're obeyed, your entire household becomes a happier place for everyone in it.

It teaches them that compliance with the boundaries produces outcomes that are positive and good.

Children who respect boundaries are the kind of children that other adults are most comfortable being around. Teachers, Sunday-school workers, summer camp counselors, and others will be grateful to you. Further down the road of life, employers and spouses will be grateful to you as well. You will have done an excellent job of raising children that behave responsibly and appropriately.

No one says this is easy! If it were easy, your tour of large department and discount stores would bring you encounters with dozens of well-behaved children, demurely walking beside their mom's shopping cart with perfect manners. The children you meet wouldn't be begging for more, grabbing things off the shelves, running several aisles away and hiding, or yelling at their mother at high volume.

As you very well know, reality is otherwise. It is difficult to manage the behavior of children. Yet here is a secret you may not have learned: As you begin to make simple, clear steps to set, monitor, and enforce boundaries, your life as a parent gets simpler and more fulfilling. When you firmly stick to your rules and make sure they're obeyed, your entire household becomes a happier place for everyone in it, and especially for you as a single parent.

Expressing Your Love

The fifth and final hallmark of effective single parenting is one in which you may already excel: Be sure that you *express your love* to your children.

Your expression of affection and unconditional love should accompany each of the four previous stages of the effective single parenting, from setting boundaries all the way through the cycle to enforcement and repetition.

Successful single parents set boundaries clearly because they do love their children! The healthy discipline of children includes monitoring of the rules as a way of showing children that someone cares about them and about their behavior. The enforcement stage occurs as an act of love. You as a parent care about your child so much that you are willing to enforce consequences as a way of helping your son or daughter learn, mature, and grow.

After enforcing a consequence, particularly with younger children, it may be useful to restate your love, while also adding that you expect a change in their behavior in the future. Doing so clarifies that you are not planning to withdraw from your children or go away because you are angry; rather, as a loving parent, you are planning to stay involved, to keep on monitoring, and to correct them as many times as needed—because you care enough to keep on helping them.

Children of divorce need to know that their parent is still going to be there. They need to know that they are loved and cared about. Whether you understand it or not, firm and clear discipline is one of the most effective ways to signal to your child that he or she is loved, cared about, and valued.

■ ■ ■ ■

Let's face it—it's much easier to ignore bad behavior than it is to correct it. Yet ignoring your children's social skills, manners, or choices is not an act of love but rather the absence of it. Do you love your children enough to care about them all the way through the cycle of effective discipline? It takes a large and generous love to expend the physical and emotional energy you'll deplete while setting the boundaries, monitoring compliance, and enforcing appropriate consequences.

Yet the results are well worth the effort. No matter how stressed your current attempts at parenting may be, it is entirely realistic and possible for you to begin by making small changes, setting a few rules, and watching your children learn to adjust their behavior: because you insist on it.

They will test, they will explore, they will try to ignore, and they may launch various levels of rebellion. As you remain patient and firm in your role as a single parent, your children will also begin to learn. When Mom makes a rule, Mom means business. When Dad sets a new boundary in the house, Dad is absolutely serious about it.

Even if your children disrespect you today, it is not too late to start gaining their respect by making small, positive changes in your management style. Sit down and decide on a few behaviors that you'd like to change. Pick only one, or select several—and start where you are.

The results may surprise you: Children learn faster than you realize. The sooner you begin to train them in the way they should go, the sooner your kids will begin to make positive changes in how they respond to you and to others.

8

How to Communicate with Your Older Children and Teens

■ ■ ■ ■

My mom and I don't talk much anymore.
I kind of miss that, but my friends say
they don't really talk to their moms either.

BRITTANY, AGE 14

Wouldn't it be nice if your teens confided in you, instead of hiding away their secrets and refusing to share their innermost thoughts?

What if you knew what your children were really thinking and feeling?

What if they began sharing their inner life with you while they were young and then kept on sharing it with you as they passed through adolescence? What if communication continued as they entered college, the workplace, and adulthood?

If you're a typical single parent, this scenario probably sounds like the impossible dream. Although many of us win the trust and confidence of our younger children—who after all need us and rely on us for almost everything—we tend to find ourselves locked out of the inner emotional world of our older children and teens, especially as they navigate adolescence and begin to form relationships and friendships, including with the opposite sex.

It has always been this way for parents, although sometimes in a two-parent household one parent gains the role of confidant and listener. In a two-parent family the children quickly learn which parent will yell at them if they share something personal, and which parent (if any) will listen patiently and then keep their secrets.

In a single-parent household, you don't have the option of offering two adults as potential counselors. There's only you! If your children don't confide in you as their parent, then of necessity they'll either hold everything inside or else find someone outside your home and family circle to talk with.

Don't you wish it were you they turned to?

Single mothers often feel estranged from their teen sons, who not only decline to share thoughts and feelings, but also often do not respect their moms. Single fathers tend to feel awkward and incompetent as their daughters reach their early teen years, not knowing what they should say or when to say it.

Although you may have kept the lines of communication open in the early years of their lives, as children grow and mature their issues tend to become more personal and their thoughts more private. Sharing "everything" with the adult who manages their schedule and controls their freedom seems like a risky option.

If I tell my dad the truth, will he make me stop dating until I'm 20?

If I tell my mom what I'm really thinking and feeling, will she freak out?

Older children and teens consider questions like this on a daily basis. As you may be discovering, they often decide to keep their thoughts bottled up inside rather than sharing them openly with you as their parent.

How did you behave at their age?

Did you tell your mom everything?

Did you give your dad a highly detailed report of all your dates?

■ ■ ■ ■

We have a friend, now middle-aged, to whom children of all ages, especially teens, tend to gravitate immediately. Within moments of meeting him, a reticent teen will pour out his darkest secrets or share her deepest wounds.

It has always been this way. Our friend has had this gift since childhood.

Not surprisingly, he is a counselor (what else?). The occupation fits his temperament so naturally that you cannot easily imagine him in some other role. Although he often counsels with adults and even seniors, this man's specialty is working with troubled adolescents and traumatized children, among whom he immediately gains confidence and quickly inspires trust.

Children and teens will tell him absolutely anything—and they do.

Having watched him over a number of years, we've managed to identify a few of his character traits that may explain this phenomenon somewhat. We aren't trying to take away the mystery of what he does—who can really figure out why others seek out this man when they hurt or suffer?—but we have watched him work, and we have discerned some of the reasons that he functions so effectively in his role as a listener and as a therapist.

A portion of the explanation can be found in a Latin phrase that forms part of the traditional giving of last rites for Catholics who are near death. The Latin phrase begins *"Te absolve peccato..."* and can be approximately translated as "I forgive you of your sins—I erase the records of your wrongs."

This man is one of the gentlest and most forgiving people we have ever known; he is this same way with everyone. While you tell him your deepest secrets it appears that he is listening intently—and yet somehow not storing up anything against you. It's as if your worst thoughts and actions don't stain this man's image of who you are. He keeps on seeing you as bright, or good, or full of potential.

You sit there, explaining to him all the horrible things you've done or said, all the evil things you've thought or imagined—and although he is absorbed in every word you speak, none of it dents his opinion of you.

How is this possible?

After you reveal the worst thing you've done, it's as if nothing was said. He smiles at you, often offering to say a prayer if you'd like. And the moment after that, it's as if you never did anything wrong in your whole life.

Life goes right back to where it was before you shared your heart: This man still believes in you, still sees good in you, still gives you hope.

Let's face it, these are the people we turn to when we need to talk: the ones who will listen to us without judging, the ones who will hear our wrongs without trying to "fix us," the ones who love us just as much at the end of our story as they did at the beginning—before they knew who we really are.

You may have someone like this in your own life: If so you are blessed. Nonjudgmental, grace-filled listeners are few and far between. You may not find any of them among your relatives or in your family circle. You may not find any of them within the pews of your church. But by the blessings of God, these people exist—and when you do find one, you will know it immediately.

You may be thinking—accurately so—that you will never become the kind of person that others confide in. Perhaps not, but you can build bridges of communication that your own children may use to cross over from their world to yours, sharing with you things you wouldn't have learned otherwise. If you will study and apply the principles outlined in this chapter, you'll be on your way to becoming a better communicator. You'll also become a better parent.

How to Talk to Your Children

There are three key things you will want to have as your aim to give to your children when you're talking with them.

Giving a Sense of Permanence

Your primary task in talking to your infants and older children should be to communicate a sense of *permanence*. Your goal is to convince them that a major part of their lives is not going to change: Your relationship with them is rock solid. It is forever; it is not going away.

What has happened to a child of divorce? She has lost her father when he left the family and moved to another home. He has lost his mother because she somehow decided to change her life. Now there is only one parent left, and the child naturally wonders if the next thing he or she will lose is you!

You need to work against that fear constantly. It is deeply rooted: Your child has experienced a shattering trauma. He trusted his parents to love him and care for him, but now one parent is gone. Will the other parent be next to leave? What happens then? Will he be all alone in the world? Who will care for him if everyone in his life runs away from him and lives in another state?

Since life has been revealed to be fragile, temporary, and full of pain, you need to constantly reassure younger children that something permanent is in their lives and readily available to them: you.

Say it as many ways as you can—you will always be there for your child! Later, of course, when he is a teenager, he may not want you to be there. He may wish you were invisible! He may insist that you drop him off two blocks away from the party, instead of driving up to the front door.

That adolescent angst is for another season of life: Right now your infant or young child needs the constant reassurance of something permanent: your love for them and your presence with them on the journey of life.

Say it and keep saying it: "I will always be here for you." Set aside your irrational fears about dying of cancer or being hit by a truck. Your potential death is a matter for the future. Right now, your task as a parent is to be a reassuring and calming presence, affirming your child with a sense of what is permanent.

Giving Confidence

Your next task in talking to your child is to give her *confidence*.

As a demographic observation, parents in Southern California tend to excel at this particular trait. California kids often grow up believing that the world is fully open to them: They can do anything and become anything. This remarkable gift of parenting may be partially a result of abundant sunshine, moderate climate, or perhaps the cool blue Pacific Ocean! But in any event, a California teen is much more likely to have self-confidence than a teen from the Northeast or Midwest.

Meanwhile, parents in all parts of the country can learn how to give their children confidence rather than instilling self-doubt or self-criticism within the minds of impressionable young children.

We worked with a man, now an adult, who was somewhat obese as a child and came to be defined by that trait. He showed us pictures: a chubby child to be sure, but not grotesquely fat. His obesity was well within childhood norms.

This man's mother called him "Pudgy" on a regular basis. It began as a nickname, but later seemed (in the growing child's opinion) to be a defining negative characteristic of his existence. He began to think of himself as pudgy, believing himself to be fat.

He sat in our office as a grown man, fit and trim, serving in the armed forces of the United States. He was in no way out of shape: His fitness was immediately obvious. Yet this man—not an anorexic or bulimic, not given to any eating disorders—sat in our office and confessed that he had always felt pudgy.

He wondered if he always would.

Another grown adult was called "Clumsy" as she matured. Sometimes the word *clumsy* was used as a noun or a name, as in "Hey, Clumsy, come over here for a minute!" At other times, the word functioned as an adjective, modifying a noun, as in "Hey, you clumsy idiot, watch where you're going!"

We sat in our office with this graceful woman, slim and reposed, whose occupation involved her in frequent hospitality. She entertained clients and the spouses and families of those clients on a regular basis. She moved among various social circles, including persons of high income and high net worth, and she did so with an articulate maturity and with evident polish.

Yet as she shared her journey with us, she revealed to us that to this day she feels clumsy much of the time: especially in a social setting. She worries constantly that she will drop a tray, spill a drink, trip and fall on the stairs, or exhibit some other behavior that will scream out to her clients and her friends, "Watch out, Clumsy is in the building!"

From all available evidence, no one else feels this way about the woman, yet this is how she sees herself—because her image of herself was molded by a parent who called her names and attacked her competence.

It is extremely easy for a mother to deprive her children of confidence, convincing a growing young boy or girl that he or she is pudgy, clumsy, stupid, or incompetent in some way. The damage may last for a season or for a lifetime. Children hear and tend to believe the images their parents use to describe them.

■ ■ ■ ■

Now let's flip the coin and look at positive parenting in action.

We sat with a junior in high school near the end of his basketball season. With one year of high-school basketball left to play, this athletic young man was already being watched by recruiters from several colleges. They would show up at his games, observe his play, and sometimes speak with him afterward—all this during his junior year, not his final year of high school.

Confident but not arrogant, this 17-year-old graciously accepted our compliments, acknowledging our awareness of his skills, including what we had observed was a deadly outside jump shot. Our conversation with him took an unexpected turn when we mentioned it.

"My mom was the first to notice that." The teen grinned. "She was coming to some of my games—as many as she could—during my first year of middle school. And one day after the game she said to me, 'Wow, you really have an amazing jump shot!' It made me feel great! It was maybe the nicest thing she ever said to me.

"I hadn't really thought about my jump shot," he continued. "I was just out there playing basketball and having fun. It was the sixth grade—our coach was also our math teacher, and I'm not sure he knew that much about basketball.

"When my mom said that, something in me kind of went, 'Yeah, I do have a good jump shot,' and that made me want to make it even better. I started working on jumpers from 10 and 12 feet. I got to where I could make those shots most of the time, so I moved back a little. Today I hit almost every 15-foot jumper I try, unless I get blocked or fouled by somebody."

> ■ ■ ■ ■ ■
>
> Hearing his mom's verdict gave the growing boy confidence in a skill that was beginning to emerge.
>
> ■ ■ ■ ■ ■

The high-school basketball player told us this quite naturally, with no trace of arrogance and no apparent flickering of self-doubt. It was if he'd said, after a compliment, "Yes, I am six-foot-two," or "Yes, I do have curly hair." Clearly, this teen's self-image included a confident awareness that he had a good jump shot. He considered this to be an established fact about himself.

The teen was correct. In the half-dozen of his games that we were privileged to attend, he did indeed nail his jump shots whenever he got within 15 feet of the basket. His shooting percentage was amazingly high.

How did this jump-shot prodigy begin to believe in his ability?

With his mother's compliment.

This mother didn't teach her son key strategies of the game of basketball. She didn't demonstrate to him how to shoot a 15-foot jumper, sometimes while off-balance, sometimes one-handed. She didn't have the knowledge of the game or the personal ability to coach him to that level of play.

What she did do—as a busy working woman raising two sons—was pay attention and notice when her child did something well. Observing his ability, she gave him a genuine, specific, highly attentive compliment. She told him that he had an amazing jump shot. (She probably meant, amazing for a sixth-grader.)

Hearing his mom's verdict gave the growing boy confidence in a skill that was beginning to emerge. Since his mom was watching, he wanted to excel even more at that particular trait. He worked on his jump shot, and regardless of how good he may or may not have been as a sixth-grader, he had deadly aim by the time he began playing varsity high-school basketball while in the ninth grade.

Seriously recruited by several colleges and universities, he chose one and led that school's basketball team to the Sweet Sixteen one year and then to the Final Four the next. He was recruited and signed by an NBA team after he completed his senior year of college.

So where do you want your son to go today?

What career—what accomplishment—do you want your daughter to achieve?

The words we use to interact with our children are powerful: They can make permanent impressions for good or for bad. As you talk with your children, make it your aim to instill confidence in them. Notice when they do something well and mention it to them clearly. Keep in mind the power of your message. If you tell them they are clumsy, they may feel that way forever. But if you tell your daughter she is graceful or has a good singing voice, what will happen?

Giving Unconditional Love

The third key trait to include in your communication is *unconditional love*.

We could have opened with this trait, of course: It is highly important. Sometimes, however, parents tend to listen past this point—believing that they already excel in this area. Perhaps they are correct.

Some parents, however, dole out generous quantities of affection and love only as long as their children are behaving in certain ways or believing certain things. When the child's preferences, choices, or behaviors begin to vary from the way the parents prefer, the well of love and affection dries up quickly.

Love becomes a commodity that must be "purchased" by the child by using the right words or living out the right behaviors. Children learn this economy very quickly: If they measure up, they are loved. If they do not measure up to the standards set by their parents, the love disappears.

Complimenting your children is a wonderful thing (see the above section), yet it is unhelpful and potentially dangerous to unite the giving of affection and love with times of achievement or success. At a subconscious level your child is learning that love is the reward for high achievement or perhaps perfection—meaning that one must always work hard for love, strive greatly, keep trying—so that love will be awarded if the child is successful in his or her goals.

Nothing could be further from the truth you are trying to instill: that your love for your daughter is unconditional and forever. It is not linked to behavior or compliance or achievement. Your undying love for your son will follow him through any and all of his life choices. He will be loved whoever he is and wherever he is, not because of any achievement but because he is your son.

With growing children, and especially with children of divorce, three of the most helpful ways to communicate with them are to assure them of something permanent, to instill in them a sense of confidence, and to demonstrate to them a love that is generous and unconditional.

Love does not have strings; love gives wings.

How to Talk with Your Teens

All of the principles above apply to interacting with your teens. If your newly 16-year-old daughter has just "lost" her dad due to divorce, your message of permanence will be health-giving for her. If your son becomes highly skilled at a computer game, notice his skill and compliment him: Maybe he'll be an air traffic controller one day, keeping you safe while you fly!

With children of all ages, including as they become teens and adults, showing your unconditional love will always be among the most helpful and most healthy ways you can communicate.

As your children become teens, there are some additional ways you can proactively communicate with them, now that they are old enough to process what you're saying and respond appropriately. With that in mind, add these options to your list of how to wisely interact with your teens.

Admitting Your Mistakes

One powerful way of reaching teens is to *admit your mistakes*. As your teens become old enough to make decisions about the use of drugs and alcohol, and as they begin to intentionally choose their own style and their own friends, as they reach the age of dating or hooking up, it may be time for you to reveal some of your own journey to them.

Parents tend to be great as preachers—telling their teens what to do and especially telling them what not to do. Parents are not always so adept at thinking back to their own teen years and admitting the mistakes they made at that time.

If you're a single mom who was sexually promiscuous during high school or college or as an early adult, there may come a time when you can share some of that journey with your daughter. You may decide to tell her, not as a preacher but as someone who lived through it, how it feels when someone says that they love you, but it turns out they only wanted a sexual hook-up, not a caring and lifelong relationship. Your focus is not so much on the outcome—which is obvious—but on how you felt at the time. Sharing your actual, unvarnished feelings from that season in your life is one of the most powerful ways you can ever bond with your older teens.

What do you wish you had known when you were a teen? What did you have to learn the hard way? If you could go back and relive your life, what are some things you would do differently, and are you really sure you could make those kinds of changes if you were that age all over again?

If you've dealt with traumas like STDs, or if you've personally had an abortion, there may be a time when it is appropriate to discuss these issues with a growing teen. You needn't be in a rush to "confess your sins" or to explain every tragic mistake or misstep that's been a part of your pathway. There are many times when it is appropriate and wonderful to simply let the past be the past.

Yet if you venture toward admitting some mistakes with your teen son, you may be surprised at how quickly your honesty "opens up" the conversation, so that it is possible to talk to him about things in a realistic, candid, up-front kind of way. Your teen daughter may not listen if you try to tell her what to do, but she will be greatly curious to know what you actually did!

Admitting that you've made mistakes humanizes you, helping your teen son or daughter relate to you as a person, not as an authority figure. This lets your relationship become based on reality, not idealism. Your teen may discover that one of the reasons you care so much about a particular issue is because you have been there, done that—and it messed up your life. That's why you're hoping they won't have to learn the same sad lesson in the same tragic way.

Relaxing Your Certainty

Another aspect of effective communication with your teen son or daughter is to *relax some of your certainty*. Teens are busy exploring the world, and they tend to consider many options, some of which may shock or surprise you. Teens value having an open mind: Most teens consider themselves open-minded and believe that they are "seeking the truth" from among competing worldviews.

When you react to a discussion with teens by slamming your certainties at them, you tend to close off conversations that might have been hugely helpful. Teens find your certainty to be a symptom of closed-mindedness. It's a turnoff; to them it means you've quit thinking about things. You are no longer a seeker of truth—you've become a narrow-minded (read, misguided) person.

No one says you have to let go of eternal truth. You need not say, "Well, I *thought* Jesus was the Son of God, but maybe he was a Martian…" As a biblical Christian, you may have core topics about which you no longer have an open mind, because the testimony of Scripture reveals Christ as God's Son and shows us that Christ died on the cross to redeem us.

Yet life gets complicated. Often our core theology is mixed up with our political preferences, our patriotic zeal, and our social and cultural convictions. We talk about God and eternal truths in the same sentence or breath as our own opinions about national events or democratic processes. We send our teens very mixed messages when we do this. We make it sound like the pathway to God is found inside a voting booth.

Instead of this, we would do very well when talking with our teens to relax our certainties and learn to become more flexible as listeners and speakers. If your daughter discovers a novel or book that makes socialism seem attractive, it may not be the best time to wave the flag and yell at her. If your son makes a random comment such as "The Goths are the nicest people in my whole school," it might not be the time to launch into a lengthy sermon against wearing black clothing.*

It is more than okay to believe what you believe. After all, you've thought about your life, you've learned from your experiences, and you've wisely chosen what you're going to support. Good for you! Now it's time for your teens to get out there and make some of these same decisions. They are much more likely to share their thoughts and feelings with you if you relax some of your certainties, listen to ideas as they are presented, and avoid rushing to judgment.

Sharing Your Feelings

A final suggestion for effective communication with teens is that you learn to *share your feelings* rather than always lecturing, teaching, and training about ideas and values. You are rarely more effective with your teens than you will be when you are honestly describing how you feel.

Teens connect well with emotions. Pay attention to the speakers that your teens tend to prefer—you'll discover that these speakers are full of passion; their emotions are very much on the surface. Adults may prefer a carefully reasoned discourse that is a correct exposition of an eternal truth, but teens often sleep through this. Yet if a speaker gets up and starts talking about her feelings—for example, her own fears, or perhaps her own anger—teens wake from their naps and begin paying attention.

It's the same way in ordinary conversation with teens. If you are

---

* Some of the least socially accepted subgroups in our society include some of the most socially accepting people you may ever meet. Can't we learn something from this? Why are *they* the compassionate ones?

building a case for what you believe—in the hopes that your teens will be won over by your amazingly persuasive skills in argument and debate—there may be no one listening but you. Most teens don't readily connect with the principles of logic. They're busy sorting out a lot of contradictory feelings as they discover their place in the social and emotional world that flows all around them.

If you pay attention to yourself, you'll discover that you often have actual feelings. Sometimes you are afraid, even now. Sometimes you get angry about things and wish you could change them. These feelings—fear, anger, doubt—are part of the life of almost every teen on this planet. When you begin to talk about your feelings, you are connecting your experience with theirs.

As you talk with your older children and teens, you may find it very helpful to admit some of your mistakes, relax some of your certainties, and talk about some of your feelings. If you do, your teens will get a look at the "real you" inside the person they know as Mom or Dad. This will help your teen daughter or son break out of the mold of always relating to you as an adult or an authority, and relate to you as a real person, someone who is much like them.

How to Listen to Anyone

Parents tend to spend a lot of time with their mouths open. That's precisely why we preceded this section with the previous two about communicating with children and teens.

To close this chapter, we'll look at some ideas about listening that are nearly universal. These concepts will apply to listening to almost anyone. You'll be able to use these three principles with your children and teens, and also with people at work, in your family, or at church.

Pay Attention with Your Whole Body and Self, Not Just with Your Ears

Have you ever tried to talk to someone, only to realize that they were staring out the window, watching a television show, or preoccupied with lint on their slacks? How did this realization make you feel? When you noticed this behavior, you probably felt like someone wasn't listening to you.

You may have been right.

Although many people insist that they can listen well "while they do this," these same people are unlikely to ever become great listeners. Who wants to talk to someone who is obviously interested in some other topic, place, or activity? Only a championship talker (and we all know some!) will keep talking when the intended listener is staring off in another direction, focused on some task at hand, or busy watching a sporting event or a television show.

Failing to "tune in" with your body language keeps you from hearing a lot of what your children and teens might otherwise tell you. If you want to hear more from them, you're going to have to learn how to listen.

To begin, make clear, nonthreatening eye contact. You are not trying to stare someone down or make them feel like they're under a microscope. Rather, you're showing them that right now they are the most important person in the world to you—and to indicate that, you are giving them your full attention. You are looking at them when they speak to you. You are paying attention.

> If you correct an error in the middle of something, then the middle may be as far as you get.

Next, be sure your body language sends the same message. Quit staring at the TV screen (why not turn it off?) and quit playing with your shoes. Turn your whole body in the direction of the person you are listening to. Make it clear that your entire self is part of the process of listening—not as if you're getting ready to pounce on the speaker, but again as if the speaker matters more than anyone and anything else in the world.

Not until you send this message will you ever begin to receive the deep, inner thoughts and feelings of most children and teens. If you are sending them signals with your body language (loud sighs are a strong signal) that you are not highly interested—they will get the message and quit talking to you.

After getting those kinds of messages repeatedly, your teens may quit trying to talk to you. At the time when they need you most, they may not even attempt to make a meaningful connection with you, believing it won't happen.

Control Your Urge to Correct What You Hear

Few things shut down a meaningful conversation faster than trying to correct, instruct, teach, or change the person you are listening to. Parents, who often feel such a strong burden to impart "the truth" to their children, sometimes end up functioning like giant bottles of white-out correcting fluid.

Do you remember when typing mistakes had to be covered up with correcting fluid? You took the cap off the little bottle and brushed white liquid over the error; the liquid dried, and you retyped the words.

Parents often function in this same way. Your child says something, and you judge the statement to be wrong. So instead of listening further, and perhaps gaining a better understanding of how your child or teen thinks, you jump in to "white out" the error and be sure your teen puts the correct words in place.

End of conversation.

Whether you are correcting a grammatical error or a philosophical one, functioning as an instructor or inspector rarely leads you to the deep places of meaningful interaction and conversation. Instead, the person you are listening to learns that it isn't safe to talk to you. What if they say something wrong? You'll jump in and try to correct them again. It's just not worth that much trouble.

Your teen may very much want to talk to you. So she tries—but instead of listening you are telling her what she should be thinking, what she should believe. You could learn so much if your mouth were shut! But there you go again. You are correcting, reproving, changing, editing, informing, and instructing her, as if she were only a very young child. Disheartened, she learns very early that there's no point in talking to you: You're just going to correct her all the time.

Your fourth-grade son wants to talk to you about something, but he isn't using correct grammar. You jump in to correct him. After all, don't you want him to learn how to speak correctly? Shouldn't he learn these things while he's young, so that he'll be respected and listened to as an adult?

How about respecting and listening to him right now?

Correct his grammatical errors when you're reviewing his homework, not when he's trying to tell you what he thinks or feels. Learn to let errors of fact, judgment, or expression sail right past you without being opposed. You'll hear more and you'll learn more. Later, at the end of the conversation, if there is a major life-threatening correction of error that simply must occur, see to it gently. But if so, wait until the end. If you correct an error in the middle of something, then the middle may be as far as you get.

Save Your Opinions for a Rainy Day (in Phoenix)

Most of us have tried to talk to someone, only to have that person continually interrupt us so that they can share their own opinion or anecdote. We're doing our best to express our feelings or tell a story, but the other person just can't stand to listen to us—he keeps interrupting to make a point of his own or to be sure that we understand how wise he is.

We tire of this quickly, so we quit talking.

You've had a conversation like that (or tried to), so remember what it feels like the next time your child or teen is talking to you. Instead of jumping in with a profound point that relates so perfectly with what your teen is saying, just wait and save it for later.

As a single parent, you can be absolutely certain that sooner or later your child or teen is going to want your opinion about something, even if it seems to be something trivial: Do you think these shoes go with this bag? But the more often you express an opinion, the less often you'll be asked for one.

One reason so many teens consider their parents to be judgmental is that when a teen begins to share her opinions or express her ideas, her mother or father interrupts her with a lengthy sermon, an oft-repeated story, or with "the answer." Although teens may very well be looking for answers, they prefer to find them through a process of discovery and exploration.

Shutting down your opinions helps the lines of communication stay open. Instead of rushing to express your intelligence, display your wisdom by waiting until a more appropriate time to express your own views.

Sooner or later your teen will say, "What do *you* think?" This may be an acceptable moment for you to express your views. Even so, you would be an incredibly wise parent if you responded by saying something like "Help me understand your question a little bit more fully. What are you really asking me?" This may lead your teen to engage in a lengthy discussion about a topic that might have been cut off, right then and there, if you'd jumped in with a quick answer.

■■■■

You'll learn more with your mouth closed and your mind open, although this may seem like a radical role reversal to you as a single parent. No one is saying that every truth is created equal, or that all opinions lead to the truth. Rather, the aim of this chapter is to make you a better listener, so that whatever is in the heart and mind of your child can be expressed by his or her conversations with you. How will you know what your child is thinking, if all you ever do is share your own thoughts?

Yet if you can learn to listen well, you may be surprised to discover that your daughter is ready to treat you like a trusted friend, confiding in you some of her deepest worries or her most troubling experiences. If your son considers you to be open-minded and available, he may sit down one evening and spend hours telling you what he truly believes and feels.

As the credit-card commercial might say: *priceless!*

Part Three

Facing the Future—Learning to Manage Your New Life

Beyond the immediate task of survival, you need to begin praying and thinking about what the future may look like for you. Should you consider a new job or perhaps a whole new career? What about going back to school and finally finishing that college degree? This part shows you how to evaluate your options realistically, how to make plans and take action steps that build a positive framework for your future, one day at a time.

We began the book by looking inward, at your personal life. We explored how to nourish your soul so that, as a healthy parent, you can care for the family that God has given you. We followed that part with a look at how to nurture your children, focusing on practical ways to adjust their behavior and build bridges of communication that connect you with their thoughts and feelings.

In this third and final major part we'll take a look at the road ahead. Will it include employment, either as a continuing career or a new one? Will you consider returning to school to gain a new skill set, certification, or degree? What will you need to know about finances and financial planning? And as we look out toward the far horizon, how can you wisely approach questions about dating and forming new relationships, including the possibility of one day remarrying?

These chapters arrive to help you move forward. Their purpose is to help you look at the concrete, daily world of single parents. You may not have wanted to join this particular club—but like it or not, you're a member now. Welcome!

Join us in the following pages for highly practical, real-life strategies about juggling job, school, kids, and finances while functioning as the sole parent in the home. Here's the good news: Others have been here before.

9

Working In and Working Out

Employment Issues for Single Parents

■ ■ ■ ■

I never wanted to have a career;
I wanted to have children.
Now that I've got both, it's mostly okay.

DIANE, SINGLE MOTHER

When his wife left him, Doug worried about the kids. Visions of an ugly custody fight flooded his imagination and haunted his dreams. What would happen to his children if his wife took them away?

As it turned out, he needn't have worried.

Abandoning not only Doug but the children as well, Doug's wife intended to start a whole new family in a different state. She'd gotten involved with a man who was moving there. When the man packed up and left, she went with him. She neither filed for nor wanted custody of the two children she shared with Doug.

Doug was relieved in the midst of his trauma. Shocked and hurting over the sudden loss of his marriage, at least he wouldn't be losing the kids!

In the next moment, he was worried again.

How could he possibly raise his children alone, working 60- and 70-hour weeks as the IT coordinator for a large bank? The long hours, and the fact that he was essentially always on call, both day and night, were prime factors in his marriage breaking up, Doug now believes. With the wisdom of hindsight, he wishes he had worked less and stayed home more often.

Could he have saved his marriage by being home? He doesn't know.

Even so, it wasn't too late for his kids. Doug was determined to be an active presence in the life of his children, ages seven and five, no matter how many sacrifices he might have to make. He began looking at his choices in a whole new light.

"I'd already lost my wife," Doug tells us with a sigh. "I wasn't about to lose my kids. They were all I had left."

■ ■ ■ ■

Doug's employer generously granted him a two-week leave of absence as he struggled to cope with his wife's sudden exit. "Of course, the office called me a lot that whole time," Doug remembers with a wry smile. "My phone was ringing at least once an hour with questions or problems. But at least I didn't have to drive in to work every day. I went in one time during that whole two weeks: an emergency."

Within the two-week period, he made a drastic decision: No matter what it took, he was ready to trade the daily commute for a work-at-home role. He relished the opportunity to drive his kids to school, pick them up later, and spend afternoons and evenings with them at home. Besides, his kids were hurting as much as he was—how do you tell your kids that their mother is running away?

During the two weeks he spent away from the office, Doug had an epiphany of sorts. No strange visions, no odd dreams—but a radical clarity in his values that had been lacking from his prior awareness.

"Before the split, I didn't get home until 7 or 8 PM," he reveals. "And since the kids were so young, that meant I was getting home pretty close to their bedtimes. I basically never saw them in those early years. I knew it was wrong, but I could never figure out how to fix it.

"When Kelly left us, my kids and I were hurting together. Every day, looking at the pain in their eyes, trying to answer questions that didn't have any answers—at least not any answers that I knew—I discovered how much I loved my kids. I realized that I'd been an absentee father during their early childhood.

"I guess in a strange way Kelly did me a favor by leaving. She helped me figure out my values and my priorities—at least the ones I hoped to have, not the ones I'd been living out for the last decade or so."

When Doug told his employer that he planned to resign, his immediate supervisor spent several weeks trying to refashion his job description so that he could continue in his same role, yet work from home. The supervisor even suggested that he might change to "consultant" status, with the potential for higher income than he had been making.

"They were wonderful, my boss especially," Doug exclaims. "But the core issue for me was that I didn't want to be such a type A, driven personality anymore. It was the only life I had ever known, but it took Kelly leaving to give me a wake-up call to get my act together. My kids and I needed to work on being together."

The first few months were awkward and difficult. Nothing about raising the kids or running the household came easily. It was new and challenging—and Doug was learning while coping with what he terms "a big hole in my heart."

Looking at his options, Doug, whose role at a large regional banking center included a heavy emphasis on computer, network, and Internet security, decided to launch his own business. Based from his home, he'd be helping other businesses evaluate and reinforce their own security challenges—that is, if he could find clients.

■ ■ ■ ■

The choice meant that instead of keeping his former income, Doug and his family would be poor while he struggled to build up a clientele and establish himself as a reliable supplier of network security.

An accomplished professional, he was nevertheless willing to learn and grow.

"When I left my job, I used the money from my vacation pay to enroll in some courses at Colorado Technical University," he explains. "They're probably the highest-rated and best-known school in the country for computer-security issues. Even though I was a working techie with a lot of experience, I still learned a lot from the courses I took at CTU. I gained some skills that I really needed."

> "I tried to listen to my boys and take them seriously. I also let them know that Dad was not going to leave them—not now, and not ever."

Meanwhile, on the job front, Doug's income plummeted.

"It was good that my kids weren't teenagers." He smiles. "The kids were so young, they didn't realize how poor we were. I didn't talk about it, and they didn't really have any way of knowing that my income had fallen off a cliff."

Doug appears surprisingly relaxed about that prospect today.

"I wasn't relaxed at all, at the time," he insists. "But I knew what I wanted to do. I was ready to make whatever sacrifices were needed."

Doug made sandwiches for his kids, both of whom were in elementary grades, and packed their lunches each day rather than giving them money for hot lunches at school. He bought clothes for his children at area garage sales and chose not to buy clothing or anything else for himself while he launched the business.

"I dressed pretty well when I worked at the bank," he admits. "I had a closet full of ties that I really enjoyed not wearing, after I quit."

Frugal by nature, Doug became much more value-conscious as his income dropped to roughly 20 percent of its former level. "We didn't need a vacation fund. My idea of entertaining the kids was taking them to softball games and soccer games. We lived near a regional park with a sports complex. We went to night games of softball leagues and afternoon soccer games of company-sponsored teams. The park was nearby and outdoors: Admission was always free. My kids don't know what 'professional' sports are."

Doug turned in his leased BMW a year early, paying a penalty to do so. He bought a Toyota Camry with more than 100,000 miles on it and drove it carefully, changing his own oil and rotating his own tires. He saved money in every category of his living expenses—paring down, simplifying, and getting by.

His one indulgence was seeing a counselor weekly. He believes he wouldn't have made it through those first few years without frequent counseling. "When I could afford to go, I went weekly," he admits. "When things got tighter, which they did, I still tried to go about once a month. It really helped me."

Doug considered counseling for his kids, but instead tried to function in that role himself. He became a counselor to his children. Competent or not, he's glad he talked freely and openly with the kids about Kelly's departure. He and the kids wept together at times; at other times he'd cope with their anger or their fears.

"Joey, the seven-year-old, was really angry and said so. Devin was quieter and I didn't always know what he was thinking. I didn't know what to do—I'm not a trained counselor—but I tried to listen to my boys and take them seriously. I also let them know that Dad was not going to leave them—not now, and not ever."

School counselors spoke with the boys as well, although not extensively. Teachers were alerted to the situation, but reported no troubling changes in the boys' behavior in the classroom or on the playground.

Doug believes it's because he was home so much, staying so plugged in to how the boys were feeling and what they were thinking. "Or maybe God just saved us from all that," he says sincerely. "I know God was helping us get through it."

■ ■ ■ ■

During the day when the boys were at school, Doug worked hard to try and build a business from scratch. Gradually, potential customers started discovering that Doug's services were useful and his knowledge of the field was current and cutting-edge. He gained a few regular clients and began to see his income rise, although still not to the level of what he'd made while employed by the bank.

About two years after he formed his own business, his former employer became a regular client, making a substantial positive impact on his business efforts.

"I already knew their system inside and out," Doug says. "I was able to reconfigure some things in helpful ways. I got a contract to manage their security, got paid on a monthly basis, and for the first time in two years there was consistency and stability in my household income, although still at a lower level."

We ask him, all things being equal, if he would make the same choices again if he were back at the moment of his wife's departure.

"Heck, yeah," he says without hesitation. "I was lonely, but I kept myself busy taking care of the kids, learning more in my field, and trying to sell my services to businesses—especially anywhere that I had a personal connection. Most of the contracts I eventually got came through knowing someone, or from a referral.

"Overall, I think the sheer necessity of trying to survive probably helped me deal with the breakup. Spending a lot of time with the kids, investing energy in trying to build a new business...I stayed busy, and that helped."

Doug's type A roots seem visible in this analysis.

His financial life worked out acceptably—eventually. Meanwhile his values changed so that a lower income did not seem like a major sacrifice. He and his children bonded in ways that hadn't been possible when he was an absentee father.

"I'm really aware of that now," he reports. "When I was married, I always told myself I was working so hard *for* the kids, and maybe there was some truth in that. But now, looking back, I wish I'd been *with* the kids a lot more when they were younger, instead of working all the time."

■ ■ ■ ■

Other single dads we interviewed expressed the same thoughts. Those with sole or primary custody of their children were more than willing to make economic sacrifices, putting career advancement aside, in order to give their children the highest priority among their values.

Would their values have shifted in this direction without the divorce?

To a man, the single dads we spoke with answered "no."

From the ashes of divorce came better fathering.

So although there is nothing in divorce to wish for, perhaps at least there are redemptive forces at work when we suffer, opening us to new possibilities and new sets of values. In Doug's case, being abandoned by his wife transformed him from a mostly absentee father into a highly engaged, actively involved dad whose love for his children anchors the other aspects of his life.

A Separate Reality: Returning to Work After a Long Absence

Responses were quite different among single mothers. Many of them were not employed outside the home when their divorce occurred. A few of our interview subjects were never married—they became single parents when the birth fathers opted not to continue a relationship. Two single moms we interviewed were widows. Their core issues of raising children and managing a household were remarkably similar to women in the other categories—women always single, or now divorced.

For the divorced women, the transition from a two-parent household to being the sole or primary caregiver was usually accompanied by an economic need to work. None of the women we spoke with during the course of this book project were financially supported (via the divorce settlement or other sources) in such a way that they could live without working. For each of them, raising the kids alone meant searching for a source of employment that would meet their needs, yet somehow leave them enough time and energy to be a full-time mom.

Finding a job like that is not easy.

Corinne's Story

Corinne describes herself as an "active" mom before the divorce, the kind of parent who attended all the school functions, went to the meetings with teachers, and visited every "open house" or similar opportunity at her children's school. In part because of that high level of activity, Corinne was on a first-name basis with many teachers and staff members in the elementary school that both her children attended.

When the divorce happened, word spread quickly at the school. Corinne, who is not the quiet or shy type, immediately began asking everyone she knew for job leads or prospects. She explained that she'd love to work close to home, and she'd prefer to work part-time if at all possible.

"You should work *here*," a second-grade teacher told her one afternoon.

An attractive idea, just not a simple one to achieve, although Corinne asked for and received the emotional and moral support of the school's principal. Being so well-known within the building helped her overcome early hurdles. Still, her employer would be the school district, not the local facility. This meant that the people who knew her were not the ones that would interview her, classify her, and assign her to a job opening if available.

"I had to apply to the school district, I had to take some tests, and they did a background check on me that took more than a month," Corinne remembers. "And when I finally got word that a job was available, they were offering me a role at a school on the far side of town, not the one that my kids attended."

Corinne passed, wondering if it was the right choice.

After two more months of waiting, turning down one further job offer from the district in the meantime, she was offered a role at her own children's school. She worked as an educational assistant, helping teachers in various ways during the school day. The position she applied for was funded at three-quarter time; later she was trimmed back to a half-time employee when both the school and the district underwent several rounds of budget cuts.

"I think the principal pulled some strings to get me hired," Corinne says in our interview. "But I didn't ask questions. I'm just glad to have work to do, and glad also that I can be at my children's school with them. Both of them rode the bus before the divorce and while I was looking for jobs. But since I got a job at their school, I've started driving every day. We all ride to school together; I stay there all day even though it isn't all 'clock' time for me, then we ride home together.

"When I feel rich, we drive through McDonald's on the way home. I get the kids apple pies or ice cream cones." Corinne smiles. "Those are the cheap things on the menu, but they're luxuries for us."

Danielle's Experience

Corinne's story resonates in the lives of other single moms.

Danielle limited her job search to a six-block area near her home and the elementary school her young son attended. She patrolled the area daily, watching for help-wanted signs in the windows of any and all businesses. When a sign went up, she walked in the door and applied for the opening, regardless of what it was.

Even so, it was many months before she found work. She often lost hope, sometimes believing that employment would never happen at all. Then one day she was hired as part-time counter help at a neighborhood bakery.

"I've already gained ten pounds," Danielle admits with a wry smile. "And that's because I control myself. I help out in the kitchen and at the counter, making and stocking cakes, pies, donuts, and breads. If I didn't control myself, I'd gain ten pounds every week! I'm learnin' a lot, and I'm tryin' to be careful."

For Danielle, having a close-to-home job is worth gaining weight for.

"My Anthony walks to the store every afternoon, when school gets out," Danielle beams. "It's about two blocks, with wide sidewalks and lots of other kids and other parents out there. I really don't worry about him; it's just a short distance and he knows the way. In fact, we live so close—less than half a mile—that Anthony knows how to walk all the way home from school."

Her son, a first-grader, walks to the bakery when the school day ends, then sits quietly (most of the time) until his mother's shift is over an hour later.

"Sometimes he gets a little crazy," Danielle admits. "But most of the time he sits there and reads, or he gets out his sketch pad and draws things. Everyone at the bakery loves seeing him come in, and of course he gets free cookies and milk!"

We ask if her employer shares her enthusiasm about her son's daily presence in the store.

"Judy's been great!" she enthuses. "She's divorced herself, so she really 'gets it' about what I'm goin' through. She told me Anthony is welcome in there every day, as long as he keeps quiet and doesn't annoy the customers."

Far from bothering the customers, Anthony seems to have become a neighborhood favorite. Regulars notice if he's even a few minutes late.

"Everybody knows Anthony," Danielle laughs. "Everybody looks out for him too. That kid won't be able to get in trouble—everybody would know about it."

In Danielle's case, the bakery's employees and its regular customers have become a second family to her and her son—a support group they definitely need as they adjust to the absence of Danielle's husband and Anthony's father.

"He ended up in prison," Danielle says softly, speaking about her ex-husband. "After he left me, he started runnin' around with some bad people. Anthony misses him, and I miss him, but I'm glad we're not mixed up in all that."

She qualifies for a minimal but helpful amount of financial aid as the parent of a "dependent child," so her bakery income is not her sole source of support. Even so, she and Anthony survive on only the basic necessities.

"I can't afford a car," she relates. "I can't afford the insurance, the license, and for sure not the gas. When Anthony and I visit my family, we take the bus. If we can't get somewhere by walkin' or takin' the bus, we don't go."

■ ■ ■ ■

Danielle's household economy is typical among single mothers we met.

At higher levels of income, the costs of living have much the same effect on single mothers, including those employed in seemingly high-paying occupations. We interviewed three single mothers who work as real-estate agents. Two of them made this choice after divorcing. The third was a licensed but inactive real-estate agent before her divorce. When her husband left her, she activated her license and went to work.

With each of these, we were hesitant to ask specific financial questions. However, based on information they freely volunteered, the highest-paid among these three women makes $40,000 a year and is raising three children. In the community she serves, $40,000 per year does not qualify her to purchase any of the houses she tries so hard to sell to other people. Instead, she and her children rent a townhome. She reports that so far she is "struggling" to keep up with her expenses.

In one form or another, most of the single moms we met used the word "struggling" to define their financial realities. No one said "comfortable" or "getting ahead financially" or "pretty well set." Many confided that they couldn't make it without the generous help, financial and otherwise, of friends and family members.

Does Working at Home Work for Busy Single Moms?

Earlier in this chapter, we met Doug, who is raising his children at home. His education and background provided him with options that are certainly not normal for most single mothers. Doug—who began with an established career and a sought-after skill set in his résumé—started a home-based business so that he could be closer to his children while they grew up.

Most single mothers do not have Doug's built-in advantages.

In spite of that, several single moms we interviewed have established, or are seeking to establish, viable home-based businesses. We'll discuss two of those in the remaining pages of this chapter.

■ ■ ■ ■

Stella was a working real estate agent when her divorce occurred. Married nearly 20 years, she was in her mid-40s when her husband left her for a younger woman. Stella had a teenager at home, plus two children nearing their teen years. Although she appreciated the income she received selling real estate, and although her hours were somewhat flexible, Stella wanted an even more home-based situation.

■ ■ ■ ■ ■

"I don't want to look back later and realize I was trying so hard to pay my bills, I forgot to love my kids."

■ ■ ■ ■ ■

She chose to become a mortgage broker, using her real-estate license and working knowledge of home loans to help her get started. Having worked for three different real-estate companies and at a total of five branch offices, Stella had many connections among real-estate agents in her city.

She used these connections as she started her business, making lots of calls (in person and by phone) on real-estate agents and branch managers. Slowly, she began to build up a good solid business selling mortgage loans.

"Business is still fairly strong," Stella volunteers. "Right now I'm getting people who want to refinance in case their home value declines. They're afraid if they don't use their equity now, they may lose some of it. A lot of them are borrowing against their homes or refinancing so that they can remodel, add on, and increase the value of their home in those ways, despite the soft market."

We ask Stella how her new business compares with being a real-estate agent, not so much financially but in terms of lifestyle and family life.

"I was away from home all weekend in those days," Stella says of her busy and successful former career. "I worked a lot of evenings too. My 'prime times' were the same times my kids were at home—which meant I was gone.

"The mortgage business is pretty much Monday through Friday, and mostly during normal daytime business hours. Although I get a lot of phone calls and answer e-mails at other times, most mortgage business still flows through banks and other lenders—and they don't work weekends, for the mort part."

Stella notices the difference.

"I have a son who's 17," she explains. "He'll be gone before I turn around. I want to have as much time with him—and with my other two—as I possibly can. Life is short—that's one thing divorce taught me. I don't want to look back later and realize I was trying so hard to pay my bills, I forgot to love my kids."

On the surface, Stella appears to be perhaps the most prosperous of the single mothers we interview during the course of this project. Stella laughs at the notion when we gently suggest it.

"All my money goes to the orthodontist," Stella grins. "Are you going to print that? As soon as my oldest got his braces off, my youngest got her braces on. I've had two kids in braces for most of the past five years. And it's not over."

■ ■ ■ ■

For another look at home-based businesses, we talked with Sherry. Her current business effort involves selling household items at group gatherings and hosted parties. Sherry was starting the business when the divorce happened. Now she hopes she can build the enterprise into something that supports her.

"I'd like to try it, at least, before I try to do something else," Sherry sighs. "I'm young enough to go back to school, or learn some new skills—but I was already doing this; now I'm just trying to do it better.

"While I was married, I was lucky if I could get one party a month. Now that it's just me and Isabel (age two) I'm scheduling two or three parties a week. If I can do that consistently—and if the orders are good—this could be a good business.

"The next six months will tell me whether this is going to work, or whether I'm going to have to find a 'real job' somewhere."

Sherry's comments introduce the perspectives we'll study in the next chapter: going back to school to complete your education, to refresh your skills, or to learn a completely new occupation. Meanwhile, we ask Sherry if her emerging home-based business is viable for supporting her and her daughter.

"Not yet," Sherry admits. "Right now we're getting along on money that my dad is giving me. Without that, my rent wouldn't be paid and my car payment wouldn't get made. But I can see how this business could generate enough income to pay all my bills right now, and maybe even to help me get ahead."

■ ■ ■ ■

Getting ahead is a common theme among single parents, both fathers and mothers. If you can get past "struggling" to "surviving" then it may be possible also to move from "surviving" to "getting ahead." Several single parents we interviewed report that a few years past the divorce, they are now beginning to see the "surviving" mode happen for them. Others freely admit that their goal is beyond merely surviving—they want to build a firm financial future for their children, even if they never remarry, even if they get to financial security more slowly than two-parent households.

Some single parents believe that if they're ever going to get further ahead, it will happen by finishing a degree, learning a new skill, or getting more education. As we'll discover in the next chapter, there's good reason to consider these options.

10

Completing or Continuing
Your Education

■ ■ ■ ■

I was 38 years old when I got my college degree.
My son graduated from high school the next year.

JANELLE, SINGLE MOTHER

Is there a gender gap in the education levels of single parents?

As we interviewed single dads for this project, every man we met had completed high school. Most had also attended technical school or received four-year college degrees. We assume that in a diverse culture such as the urbanized United States in the early twenty-first century, there must be single fathers who have dropped out before finishing high school—yet we met no one at all in this category. In fact, several of the single dads we interviewed held postgraduate degrees in professions such as engineering, computer science, and forensics.

By contrast, we met single moms who did not complete high school, including one inspiring young woman whose story we'll share in this chapter. We also met single mothers who finished high school but never went on to further study. Still others attended college for a few semesters before dropping out. Single mothers with four-year university degrees were also among our interviewees.

Although we met highly professional, highly accomplished single moms, the overall difference in education levels between the men and women among our interview subjects raises the question of a substantial gender gap among single parents. Women seem much more likely than men to lack formal or completed education. No single mothers we interviewed held postgraduate degrees.

This disparity may be somewhat driven by the fact that, since the woman bears the child, she is much more likely to end up raising the child. And with women bearing children at earlier ages, including during their own "childhood," there may be logical explanations for some portion of the apparent gap in educational levels among single dads and single moms.

Nonetheless, we concluded our project by wondering why so many single fathers complete their education before parenting chores occur, whereas so many single mothers struggle to balance raising their children with the completion or continuance of their education, even at the high school level.

We have no answer, yet the question is highly compelling.

For the present time, let's look at some of the options open to single parents who believe, often rightly so, that further education will help them establish a stronger financial base for their children and family, or will help them achieve personal and career goals that are meaningful to them.

We'll begin at the earliest educational level reflected in our interviews, with a single mother whose parenting began before she completed high school. Her story is a great example of how learning can increase not only our employment options and prospects, but also our self-confidence.

Chelsea: Celebrating Her GED

Chelsea's long-term relationship (19-plus months of a "steady" romantic involvement) ended when she learned she was pregnant. The baby's father, himself a high school student, denied responsibility for the child and urged Chelsea to get an abortion. Although usually unreliable when making promises, especially financial ones, the young man did offer to pay for the abortion himself.

She hesitated for a long time before choosing to keep her baby. She considered having an abortion, yet somehow the choice didn't feel right to her. "It seemed like I would be killing my baby," Chelsea explains. "Maybe I shouldn't feel that way, but that's how it seemed. I just couldn't do it."

She also strongly considered planning an adoption. She watched an older sister choose adoption as a teenaged mom. The sister returned to a "normal" life after giving birth—going on to attend a nearby college, begin a career, get married, and start a family of her own. Chelsea saw many positive outcomes in this possibility, but she still felt strongly connected to her child.

"I don't know why I kept my baby," Chelsea tells us, appearing near tears as she speaks, "but it felt like the baby was part of me. I didn't want to be separated from my baby, even if it made my life hard."

Looking back, she admits that life was definitely hard.

Living at home with four siblings, the young mother found herself getting up all night to feed and care for her infant daughter, then often falling asleep during the day at high school. Although a bright student, her grades began plummeting.

"I couldn't stay awake in class," Chelsea recalls. "I'd take my baby home after school, my house would be crazy, then my baby would keep me up all night long, crying or fussing or waking me up."

Her high school did have an active program for teen mothers.

"I took my baby with me to school," she sighs. "I could have kept on doing that, but I needed money. I wanted my baby to have things. I wanted to have things for myself. There was nobody to help me: just me."

Chelsea chose to drop out of high school before finishing her junior year, even though the school's day-care center was a positive experience for her child. She knew that others considered her choice a mistake—for her, it was all about the money.

When a new coffee shop opened a few blocks from her house, Chelsea saw a sign on the door that they were hiring. "It was in a bad neighborhood," Chelsea says as she describes the area. "Then they knocked some stuff down and built some new stuff, including the coffee store. Everything looked a lot better after that."

Nervous about her first interview, somehow it wasn't as bad as Chelsea had expected. She was offered a part-time job at the coffee shop, working afternoons and evenings. She soon discovered that she enjoyed working, she enjoyed meeting people, and she even enjoyed drinking coffee.

"That surprised me," Chelsea laughs. "I never drank coffee before I got my job. I would do a hot cocoa or something when me and my friends went out for coffee, which wasn't very often. Back then, I didn't like the taste of coffee!"

Energetic, enthusiastic, and outgoing, Chelsea succeeded in her role as cashier, coffeemaker, and store helper. In less than six months, she was offered a chance to become a full-time employee. With her mother available to watch the baby when needed, Chelsea said yes to the promotion. She was 18 years old.

"They told me I had the right attitude," Chelsea relates. "I think they meant I was friendly to the customers. I really like the customer part. I like knowing people's names. I like knowing what they're gonna order."

■ ■ ■ ■

Chelsea began working full-time; the higher income and good benefits gave her a strong sense of personal accomplishment and satisfaction. Working at the coffee shop also led to an opportunity to complete her high-school education.

"Some people at the store decided to go to college," Chelsea recalls. "There was a company program where they paid for classes, and a lot of people took a class or two. Why not? It was all free."

Talking to a district manager for the coffee chain, she decided she would study for her GED, then take the test. It was a return to her bright-student heritage; as she began to prepare for the GED she realized she missed learning.

"I was kinda nervous at first about taking the test," she admits. "But the more I studied, I kinda realized, *I know this stuff!*" Her test score confirmed her brightness, and she passed the GED on her first attempt.

"My mom had a graduation party for me," she says with a huge smile. "She bought a cake, and some of my coffee friends came, plus some of my school friends from when I was in high school. It was a lot of fun! I was proud of myself."

We ask Chelsea about her educational future.

"I'm gonna take some college classes when my baby goes to school," she explains. "If I'm still working here, the classes will be free. Right now I'm just glad I finished high school; I've got a piece of paper to prove it!"

Blessed with a mother willing to do daily child care, Chelsea's options may be less limited than most. Yet her story illustrates the fact that even a teen mom can find a way to complete, continue, or pursue her additional education. No one is suggesting that any part of the process is easy, yet going back to school can lead to a strong sense of success and satisfaction—a useful counterpart to the daily struggles and many difficulties of raising your kids alone.

Day-care centers for unwed mothers are commonplace in urban high schools; you might be surprised at the extent to which rural, remote school districts now offer similar services and programs. It's a case of the educational system adapting to an emerging trend in our culture—teens having children and keeping them.

In the heated battle over abortion, not everyone stops to realize that the choice of life—bringing a baby to term and keeping it—usually involves a high level of personal sacrifice on the part of teen mothers. It often also involves the active participation of that mother's own parents and family, an extended support network that will probably be called upon to make many sacrifices in the interest of raising the new child. Allowing a baby to be born—then keeping it—is a beautiful, compelling, and morally wise choice, but it is rarely an easy one.

Ramona: Achieving an Associate of Arts Degree

Ramona's story parallels Chelsea's experience in several important ways. She was sharing an apartment with her boyfriend and six-month-old son when the boyfriend abruptly abandoned them both. Six months of listening to a baby cry all night—her son had colic and other problems—may have driven him away, she believes.

"Both of us got no sleep at all," Ramona says about those difficult days. "So both of us kept getting mad at each other all the time. We were fighting a lot, mostly about nothing. We didn't plan to get pregnant; we didn't plan to be parents. It just happened."

Ramona, who had not worked after her son was born, could not afford to pay the rent on the apartment, let alone manage the utility costs. "Our cable bill was about $100 a month," she remembers. "Marcus had every sports channel there was, every pay-per-view sports thing, like boxing. When he left, he was two months behind on paying the cable bill. They shut it off right after that."

Ramona did the only thing she could think of—she packed up her infant son and moved back in with her parents. They seemed glad to receive her. They even remodeled a downstairs bedroom so that she could share a room with her baby.

She cried a lot in those days.

"I missed Marcus, I missed living on my own, I felt sorry for myself being trapped with a fussy baby all the time. I kind of hated the whole world."

Eventually her father had a talk with her.

"I don't know what Mom was thinking, but Dad sat down with me one day in the kitchen, on a weekend, and we had a long talk. Dad told me if I wanted to go to community college—it was six blocks away—he and Mom would take care of Andrew while I was at class."

A high-school graduate with a few college credits from a special program during her twelfth-grade year, Ramona gave serious thought to returning to school.

"I ended up doing it to get away from my baby," she confesses. "I was going crazy—I would have done anything to get out of the house. So when Dad talked to me about college, it didn't take me long to decide."

With the support of her parents, Ramona enrolled for the next term, finding classes that were held in the afternoons and evenings. "I'm not a morning person," she tells us. "I didn't even look at classes before eleven o'clock."

An adviser at the school helped Ramona choose courses that would yield the shortest possible path to a completed degree. About 18 months after her first day of class, in part

> ■ ■ ■ ■ ■
>
> "My parents had a big party for me...They celebrated like I'd just won *American Idol* or something."
>
> ■ ■ ■ ■ ■

because she had previously earned some college credits, Ramona was awarded an associate of arts degree in business.

"My parents had a big party for me," Ramona grins. "They celebrated like I'd just won *American Idol* or something. They invited everybody. They filled the whole house with all these relatives I don't even know. But everybody gave me presents. Some people even brought presents for Andrew."

Ramona's parents did not require or push her to work while she was in school.

"They told me I could live there without paying rent, as long as I was going to classes and working on a degree," she remembers. "So that was a big reason to stay in school and finish my program. Plus, they were paying for my books and all my classes anyway."

■ ■ ■ ■

Two months before receiving her AA, Ramona was offered a job that would begin after the completion of her program. She would be working in the credit-card services department of a major corporation centered in her city. Counselors at her community college helped connect her with the job. They also helped her prepare a résumé and a cover letter when contacting the employer. In addition, counselors at the college helped her prepare for the interview session, conducting mock interviews to show her what the process would probably be like.

Then came the fateful day—her first actual employment interview.

"I was nervous," Ramona says. "I thought I'd flunked the whole thing. There was no way I was gonna get that job, but then they hired me."

Nearly three years later, Ramona is still employed by the same company. She and her son are still living in her parents' basement. Her parents have remodeled again, adding a mini-kitchen and enlarging a downstairs family room for her use.

"It's almost like having my own place." She smiles. "Except it's a lot cheaper. I'm helping them with utilities and I'm buying my own groceries, but they still aren't charging me any rent, even though they could."

Ramona's parents are talking about helping her buy a house, a thought she appreciates but is not quite ready to consider.

"I know it's a smart thing," she says. "But right now Andrew loves his grandparents so much! He's with my mom all day while I'm at work. I'm gonna wait until he's in first or second grade before I really think about buying a house. That way he'll be in school all day.

"Plus," she adds as an afterthought, "I think I'd like to stay real close to Mom and Dad even after I move. That way Mom can still take care of Andrew in the afternoons if he gets out of school before I'm done at work."

For Ramona, the completion of an associate of arts degree has brought a career that is financially rewarding for a young woman in her early 20s. Although we don't ask for economic details, she volunteers.

"I'm making $2218 a month," she tells us. "And sometimes we get bonuses for meeting our goals in the department. So that's extra. And I'm thinking about selling jewelry on the side. I have a friend who's doing that."

Living rent-free at home in a city located in the Midwest, Ramona's income is much more than adequate for her needs. Volunteering information again, she explains to us that she's banking as much as she can, putting money away for Andrew's future.

"I've got more than $10,000 in the bank right now." She beams. "And I still spend way too much money on my clothes!"

Ramona's employer, who has a partnership with the community college she attended, prefers to work with AA-degreed applicants as opposed to those with only a high-school education. For Ramona, achieving the associate's degree literally opened the door to what is, for her, a rewarding career.

"I may work here forever," she tells us. "It's a good company with a lot of benefits. My parents say I'd be crazy to leave, and I don't see why I'd want to."

We ask her if she thinks about marriage.

"Someday…maybe," she says slowly. "I feel like I've been married once, even though Marcus and I weren't actually married, not legally I mean. So I feel like I've been married and it didn't work out.

"I have two good friends that are married, and their lives don't look any happier or any better than mine," she concludes. "I guess if the right guy comes along, why not? But I'm not even dating right now. I've got a good job, my son is growing into a beautiful little man, and I'm happy with the way things are."

Kendra: Degree Completion for Busy Working Adults

"My mom and I got divorced within two months of each other," Kendra remembers. "It was kinda weird. Both of us got married almost at the same time too—Mom's third marriage and my first.

"My mom and I kinda do everything together, for some reason…"

Kendra, the mother of two young sons, experienced the reverse of Chelsea and Ramona's situation—her mother moved in with her.

"Mom didn't have nowhere to go." She shrugs. "I was in an upstairs duplex, right by a park. I didn't wanna move: My kids loved playing in that park."

Kendra, whose divorce was simple and uncontested, welcomed her mom with open arms—at least at first. Her two-bedroom apartment was large and light, with oversized windows and nice (for an urban area) views.

"Mom said she didn't know what to do," Kendra recalls. "I told her to move in with us, my boys love her anyway. It worked out good at first, before she started getting on my nerves."

Although their relationship is generally friendly, Kendra and her mother fought a lot after the "honeymoon" experience wore off. Both women were used to running their own households and doing things their own way. Neither woman wanted to compromise or back down.

"I finally told her—it's my house, and these are my rules," Kendra declares. "It was kinda fun to say that to her too!"

Her mom got the picture. After that, the two of them settled into a more peaceful routine. Her mother, who has rarely worked in her adult life, showed no interest in looking for a job. Once Kendra realized her mom was going to be around the house most of the day, she began thinking about going back to school.

"I had almost two years of college credits," she says. "I went to the U, then I went to a community college. But when I went back to school, I ended up at a private university up north—they have this degree-completion thing for busy adults. That way I could keep on working. I needed to keep my job; I was the only one making any money!"

The pattern was similar to the one that existed during Kendra's marriage. Throughout the nearly ten-year period during which she was married, Kendra's warehouse job in the beverage industry was the household's principal income, often its only income. Dillon, Kendra's husband, who battled alcoholism and occasional drug use, found it difficult to hold on to a job once he obtained one.

Kendra herself brings up the similarities.

"It was like I got married to my mom," she laughs quietly. "I was right back where I always was, the only one working, the only one bringing home a paycheck. I got tired of that, but at least I was used to it…"

For Kendra, there was good news in the positive way that a private university approached the completion of her education as a busy working adult. "They looked at my total job history," she tells us. "I had been a shipping clerk, then a security guard, then I moved upstairs to human relations. The school gave me credit for a lot of my work experience and my life experience, plus I did have almost two years of college from before I got married."

Kendra took night classes, driving about ten miles one way to the university campus, and completed a bachelor's degree in business, with a major concentration in human relations, in just 15 months.

"The company paid for all my classes and my books," she relates. "My mom was back home watching my boys. So all I had to pay for was the gas to go back and forth to school. Then, I had to figure out when to study."

Kendra discovered that her on-the-job life related significantly to the courses she was taking. "The things I was learning at school were just like the things I was dealing with at work," she says. "So in that way it was easier; it wasn't like I was studying airplane mechanics at night or something. My homework was almost always the same kind of problems that I deal with every day, in my real life."

■ ■ ■ ■

Kendra completed her degree, put on a robe and hat, and graduated.

"My girlfriends from work came," she smiles. "And my supervisor was there; she's a very professional woman with a master's degree. My boys yelled when they heard my name, and that was kinda fun. Everybody in the whole place heard my boys screaming for me."

Kendra's friends took her out to dinner for a celebration, then her life went right back to normal, except in one respect.

"My mom got married again—for the fourth time—right after I graduated from the university. I was like, wow, I got that done just in time!"

She laughs openly.

"I'm glad to have her out of my house!" she exclaims. "Mom, if you're reading this, no offense! But I'm glad to have my life back."

In the next breath, Kendra changes her view.

"There's no way I could have got my degree, though, without Mom being there for my kids, being there for me," she admits. "I don't know who would have watched my boys while I went to school. I don't think I would have even considered a program like that, except Mom was at home anyway, right there in the house."

Is there a major difference in her life, now that she's earned the degree?

"Yes and no," Kendra says thoughtfully.

"My supervisor has been really supportive of me this whole time. She's the one who brought it up in the first place. She wants to train me for management; she says I have a bright future. But right now—right this minute—I'm doing the same job, making the same pay, everything is just like it was before I took those classes."

Kendra thinks for a moment.

"One thing has changed though," she continues. "I feel a lot better about myself, on the inside. Having a college degree, from such a good school, makes me feel like I've accomplished something, like I've done something I can be proud of.

"It makes me feel better about myself, and I think it makes me a better example for my boys too. I want both of them to go to college!"

Advanced Degrees or Skill-Based Training

Trina's husband abandoned her, returning to the country of his birth. Fleeing his marriage and his family, he left behind a young wife with a high-school degree, plus three very young children.

"I didn't know what to do," Trina says softly. "It was really awful."

Trina found help from an unlikely source: her husband's extended family. "We were living with them anyway (during the marriage)," Trina sighs. "But I thought they would kick me out when Cesar left."

Instead, her husband's parents told her they would care for her kids while she pursued a job or went back to school. She was welcome to live there "forever," according to her husband's mother.

"We were still married," Trina says of that moment in history. "But I didn't know if he was coming back. It really surprised me when his family just took care of me, took care of my kids, took care of everything."

She considered everything, but mostly she wanted to learn a trade. Beyond that, she wanted to learn it as quickly as possible.

"I couldn't see going to school for four years," she relates. "It would take too long, my kids were growing up. I needed to learn how to do something, then I needed to start making money."

Trina found a cosmetology program that was nine months long; most similar programs took longer to complete. "That's what sold me," she says with a smile. "It was like having a baby: nine months. I thought I could handle that."

Trina, still legally married but functionally divorced, found that she enjoyed learning a new skill. When the time came for licensing and exams, she wasn't even worried.

> The extended family is a healthy, mostly happy environment. "I like knowing my kids are safe," Trina says. "...It's like everybody takes care of them."

"I knew what I was doing." She beams. "I knew I would pass. And more than that, I knew I could make good money at this—which I am."

She continues to live with her husband's relatives. The extended family is a healthy, mostly happy environment. "I like knowing my kids are safe," Trina says. "They've got uncles and cousins, they've got grandparents, it's like everybody takes care of them; everybody makes sure they're okay."

Trina's husband has since made contact with his wife, telling her he does definitely plan to file for a divorce. All the same, it hasn't happened.

Trina, who strongly suspects her husband is living with another woman, says she won't file to end her marriage. "If he wants a divorce, he's gonna have to come back here and get one," she says firmly. "He's gonna have to look at me, and look at his kids, and see what he's missing."

We included Trina in our project because in everyday life she functions as a single parent—though for that matter so do thousands of military wives while their husbands are serving on overseas assignments. The difference is that a military wife generally receives her husband's paycheck during his absence from home. Trina receives nothing at all from the man who is still, legally at least, her husband.

Attending a trade school, achieving a license, then seeking and finding a job, Trina is proud of what she earns in wages and tips.

"I work every other Saturday," she tells us. "I hate being away from my kids, but the money is great on Saturday—that's when everybody comes in."

∎∎∎∎

During the course of this project, we met with single mothers who have taken classes to achieve a real-estate license; others who have gone back to school at nearby technical or community colleges. One ambitious single mom is working on an MBA degree that she hopes will open the doors to a higher-paying career.

"I'm all I've got," Sarah explains. "Whatever my family is going to have, I'm the one who will earn it for us. So I'm doing everything in my power to get an MBA from a good school, then use it to find a better job."

Sarah takes all her classes online.

"I don't leave the house." She smiles. "I study at night after work. There are two times a year—only two—that I actually have to be on campus. So far those times have worked out okay."

∎∎∎∎

Consistently, single moms evaluate their lives and their choices on the basis of how the education they seek, if any, will affect their children. If overall it seems to be a net gain for the family—short term or down the road—single mothers will make whatever sacrifices are necessary to get ahead.

Chelsea, whose story we told at the beginning of this chapter, is a prime example of this phenomenon. Working hard right now, waiting until her daughter is of school age, she plans additional education when the time is right for her family. Like many of the single moms we met, Chelsea tends to think of her daughter first when making decisions about employment or education.

Are the children of single parents deeply loved and greatly cared about?

Our survey says *yes*.

11

Money Matters

Financial Reality and Your
Life as a Single Parent

■ ■ ■ ■

When I grow up and get a job,
I'm gonna take my mom to McDonald's.

CALEB, AGE 9

When you think about what it means to be a single parent, do you picture someone like Donald Trump?

Probably not.

Not that Trump hasn't been single from time to time—it's just that most of today's busy single parents are never quite in Trump territory, financially speaking. They struggle to pay their bills. They rent apartments rather than owning their homes. A surprising number of them share housing with a family member or with a close friend.

We've been working with single parents, both mothers and fathers, for more than two decades. Once in a very long time we'll meet a single father whose income or employment puts him in the category of "reasonably comfortable." Such dads are very few and far between.

So far, we haven't met a single mother whose financial status places her in an upper-income bracket. Such moms may be out there, perhaps in Hollywood? But we haven't met one yet, not even as we spent three years conducting research and interviews for this book project. Single mothers may be among the lowest-income demographic groups that we've studied. Most of them are just barely getting by—surviving, but not making much economic progress.

This is partly a function of the fact that single mothers tend to be young; often they begin having children before they have a chance to enter the work environment and seek a steady job. They may rely on a husband's income during their marriage; when the husband goes away, so does the income.

We met with several single fathers who reported that their ex-wives appear to be substantially better off than they are—a reversal of the sort of roles one might expect. Most of the single moms we interviewed surmised that their ex-husbands are about as poor as they themselves are, with some exceptions. "He still has his same job," one single mom said of her ex-husband. "But I don't think he has any more money than we do."

If you're a single parent who is experiencing poverty, take some comfort in the fact that other single parents live in similar worlds.

"What we can't handle," one single mom told us as she described her family of three, "is when something major happens—like car trouble. There's just no margin; we don't have anything in the bank. We can't take care of ourselves if there's a big emergency and we need money fast."

A lot of single parents feel the same way.

In this chapter we'll look at ways to approach this challenge, borrowing ideas and strategies from single parents who are finding their way through the difficult landscape of constant poverty.

The Unpleasant but Necessary Task of Making a Household Budget

We heard it from three single parents who are moving forward in an economic sense: The first step is definitely the most difficult.

"You have to make a budget," Samantha shares early in our interview. "Without a budget you don't have any idea where your money is going, you just look around and it's gone. I think that's normal for most of us, but until you know where your money is going, there's no way to feel like you have any control."

Samantha is big on control, but she learned her lessons the hard way.

"I was the poorest person I knew, and I was trying to raise my three kids," is her assessment of her postdivorce finances. "I wasted a lot of time looking around and resenting people who seemed to have more money than I did, which was basically everybody I knew.

"I was surprised—I still am surprised—at how few people ever tried to help me out in a financial way. People would say things like 'Let me know if you need anything' but do you know how hard that is to actually do? What am I supposed to say back to them—that I need $500 to help pay next month's rent?"

She shakes her head. "I wasted a lot of time feeling sorry for myself, and then one day I realized that no one was going to help me. So I sat down and tried to figure out where my money was going. It didn't work."

Samantha decided to write down all her expenses for a week. She kept a pen and a small spiral notebook in her purse. Every time she spent money she recorded it in the notebook.

"I didn't count things under a dollar," she says. "So if I bought a can of Coke out of a machine, or if I bought a newspaper, I didn't count that."

After a week of tracking each expense item, Samantha stared at the sheets of paper in her notebook and decided she could do it for another week, making the same decision when that week ended. When a new month started, she decided to track every expense she had for that whole month.

"When you do it for a month, you can really see what's going on," is how she summarizes her experience with tracking expenses. "I didn't learn much from doing it for a week, but when I sat down and literally wrote down every expense for a month, that was the start of my new life, financially."

Samantha discovered two major items of expense in her life: gasoline and babysitting.

"I didn't realize how much I was paying to have people watch my kids." She shrugs. "I was working, so I couldn't be home to watch them myself. When I saw how much it was for a month, the total shocked me!"

Samantha was equally shocked by her monthly total for gasoline.

"My gasoline for the month cost more than my car insurance, and I was paying a lot for car insurance," she remembers. "I had a few speeding tickets on my record and my insurance rates were pretty high. I couldn't believe that I actually spent more for gasoline in a month than I spent for insurance."

By tracking each expense for a calendar month, she realized there were four major categories for her expenses: housing costs, food, gasoline, and babysitting.

"Almost everything I spent was in one of those four categories," Samantha says. "It's not like I was going out to movies or buying clothes for myself. My money was going to pay rent and utilities, buy food, buy gas, and pay sitters."

She added up the total expenses in each of those four areas and then began to make decisions that she says were difficult. "What could I cut back on?" she asks us rhetorically. "I wasn't wasting any money. I didn't have any to waste!"

Still, she knew she had to make some cuts—a realization she says did not occur until she was looking at the budget numbers in black and white, listed on a sheet of paper in front of her.

"I know a lot of people use computers," she admits. "But my budgeting was done with just a notepad and pen. Then at the end of that first full month, it was a single sheet of paper with columns of numbers on it. I used a calculator to do it, not a computer."

■ ■ ■ ■

Samantha decided to try to reduce babysitting expenses and also cut back on gasoline expenses. She didn't know if it would be possible.

"I started asking people if they could watch my kids for a morning or an afternoon, or maybe a whole day," she says. "A friend of mine who had two kids of her own, who was home all day, decided she could take my kids one day a week. In return, I would take her two kids sometime during each weekend. I got the better part of the deal: She had my kids all day, but I usually just had her kids for a few hours. So maybe it wasn't fair for her, but it really helped me a lot—that saved me one day of babysitting money."

Samantha's stepmother also signed up to take the kids for one day each week. It was a big decision for the 58-year-old stepmom to make, but it helped Samantha cut another day of babysitting expense out of her regular weekly budget. Her stepmom insisted on watching the kids for free.

"Every single mother should know exactly where her money is going," Samantha asserts.

"I went from paying for five days of babysitting every week down to just paying for three days," Samantha says. "That was almost like getting a nice raise! The first week that happened, I was amazed at how much money I saved."

Then she attacked her other category of high expenses.

At work, she posted a note on the bulletin board looking for someone who was willing to consider ride-sharing. She discovered a co-worker who liked to drive, and who was willing to pick her up every day and take her to the office. The new arrangement seemed to work well for both.

"Before that I used about a tank of gas to go from Monday to Friday," Samantha says. "And that was costing me about $40 most of the time. Barb—my co-worker—was willing to pick me up and drive me to work, and she only wanted $20 in gas money per week. That meant I could save $20 each week by letting someone else drive. To me, that was a lot of money."

Samantha admits that she didn't adjust well to being a passenger.

"I'm glad you're not using my real name for this," she tells us, wrinkling her nose. "That way I can tell you that it drives me crazy to ride with Barb to work. She's a very cautious, very slow, very careful driver. I can't stand it sometimes! But I tell myself that I'm saving $20 a week."

For Samantha, these savings began to add up quickly.

"It was almost as good as my getting a second job," Samantha claims. "Which I had thought about doing sometimes, but how could I? I didn't see my kids enough as it was. And I would have had to get more child care if I took a second job, which would have meant more money for babysitters."

Instead, by looking at a budget sheet and seeing where her money was actually going, she realized she could trim her expenses in ways that were practical and immediate.

"Every single mother should know exactly where her money is going," Samantha asserts. "If you don't know that, start finding out right away. Keep track of everything for a month, then sit down and look at it.

"You may be surprised by what you find out. I know I was."

Develop an Emergency Fund

You've heard it before—a small amount of savings, almost any amount, adds up over time. If you're like most single parents, you're sure you don't have any money that can be saved. You need everything you have just to pay your bills.

Nadia argues otherwise.

"I didn't get anywhere financially until I started putting $10 a week in my savings," she says. "That was the first time I started feeling like I was being smart with my money. I started having hope that things would get better."

Nadia opened a share savings account at her credit union. She was already having her paycheck sent to the credit union by direct deposit. She opened a new account, savings only, and each week she transferred $10 from her checking account over to the new savings account.

"It was hard to do that the first few weeks," she says. "I would look at that money and think—*I need that!*"

In spite of the difficulty, she persevered.

"When it got up to $50, I was really proud of myself," she remembers. "And it got easier to just put the money over there every week after that."

We ask Nadia about the first time she dipped into the fund.

She remembers it with clarity.

"I got the balance up to about $350. Which to me was a big amount of money. And right about then, my son went to the dentist, and I had to pay part of the costs.

"Anyway, I took the money out of the savings account, put it in the checking account, and paid the dentist. I was so proud! And I thought—*I couldn't have done this unless I had a savings account to fall back on.*"

We ask Nadia how much her savings balance is today, if she's comfortable sharing the amount with us.

"About $82, I think," she says. "I just paid my car license for this year. Before I started saving I wouldn't have had the money to do that. Now I just take the money out of savings, put it in checking, and pay the bill."

Although Nadia hasn't built up thousands of dollars in the bank, she's managed to do something even more important. She's created a cushion of cash that is available for those sudden emergencies that plague any household, not just ones that are headed by single parents.

It's one of the wisest financial strategies we've learned from a single parent, and it's something almost anyone can achieve.

"I've thought about putting in more than $10 a week," Nadia tells us. "But right now that's still a lot of money for me. And it's working out really well. I don't know how it happens, but about the same time I get a high balance in there, all of a sudden we need the money."

Since needing money is a constant reality for single parents, it's an extremely wise decision to save a small amount each week in an emergency fund.

The Credit-Card Trap

Although we avoid asking highly intrusive financial questions, many single parents volunteered information about their credit-card use. For the ones who told us about credit cards, it was usually a love–hate relationship.

"If the grocery story didn't take Visa, my kids wouldn't eat," is how one stressed-out single mother told us about her use of credit. "I make sure that I send in the payment every month so my card doesn't get cut off.

"I'm completely serious. If Albertson's didn't take credit, I don't know how my children would have any food to eat."

Other single parents told us the same thing about gasoline.

"I put all my gas on credit," one single father confessed. "Where else is that money supposed to come from? I don't make enough money to fill up the tank, especially not at today's prices! My credit-card balance just keeps getting higher and higher, but what am I supposed to do? Stop buying gas?"

It seems impossible to live in today's world without maintaining at least one active credit-card account. Single parents, whose income may not match up with the needs of their household, are especially vulnerable to the trap of putting daily living expenses on a credit card—day after day, week after week.

"What else can I do?" one single mom asked point-blank. "I'm not happy about it, but I really don't have any choice."

Single parents seem resigned to their fate as users of credit. Striving to be as responsible as possible, many single moms end up putting gasoline, clothing, household supplies, groceries, and other items on credit cards. The result is a credit balance that grows higher and higher. Adding insult to injury is the high rate of interest that the new balance incurs. With the best of intentions, many single parents are falling further and further into debt with the passing of each new month.

There are no easy answers. While most single parents we interviewed on this topic seemed to regard their continuing credit use as a "phase," many were candid enough to admit that they couldn't imagine paying off their credit cards any time soon, if ever.

"I don't see how, I really don't," one single mom confessed.

The simplest tricks may be the best: Leave the credit card at home, forcing yourself to either pay cash for your shopping trip or else forgo the purchase. If you convert even one transaction a week from a credit-card purchase into a cash transaction, you'll be making a small step in a very positive direction.

Let's face it—most of us tend to spend less when we're spending cash. It's entirely too easy to just slide a card through a machine and spend money without actually "feeling it." Somehow when you peel those $20 bills out of your purse or wallet and hand them to a cashier, you have a much deeper sense of how costly your shopping trip has become. You are likely to cut back, eliminate a few items, and go without a few things rather than running your credit-card bill higher.

This kind of economizing, at the grocery store or the discount store, can help you quit going further into debt, or can at least slow down the rate at which you are going further into debt.

Meanwhile, if you've built up a pattern of saving in an emergency fund, you may be able to take larger sums of money out of that account from time to time, making large payments against a credit-card balance you already have. When you can send in $300 instead of making the minimum payment due, you begin to make progress against paying off the accumulated debt you owe.

Few accomplishments in life bring as much satisfaction as paying off a credit-card balance in full. If you can pay off a credit card and maintain the balance at zero, paying off your purchases each month as you go, you will be managing your credit instead of having your credit manage you. You'll save money every month in interest and carrying charges, and you'll feel confident of your financial management abilities.

The Debit-Card Trick

One of the simpler ways to wean yourself from credit cards is to switch to using a debit card instead. Many debit cards are branded with global names, making them almost as simple to use as regular credit cards, and in nearly as many places.

Debit cards offer the additional protection of requiring a PIN, making it harder for a thief to steal your card and then use it. In this way debit cards can be safer than carrying regular plastic.

When you choose to use a debit card your transaction seems much like it was before—swiping a card through a scanner or machine— yet now you are spending your own money out of your checking account, rather than piling up new debts. Spending your own money tends to make you a bit more conservative. After all, you don't have much money. Accordingly, you tend to be careful and thrifty when spending it.

A word of caution—it's easier to overdraw a checking account when you use a debit card. If you tend to always have a low balance— which you probably do—it can be easy to accidentally overdraw your account when using a debit card to make a lot of small transactions. By the time you sit down and enter all the receipts into your checkbook register, it may already be too late. You may have overdrawn your account without even realizing it.

To avoid this problem, have your savings account set up so that it covers or cushions any overdraft in checking. Even if you only manage to have $50 in your emergency savings fund, that amount would prevent a $6 overdraft from happening. You want to prevent overdrafts because many banks now charge $25 or more per overdraft, meaning you could quickly owe $75 or $100 in fees as a result of a few small overdrafts.

If your bank allows you to link the savings account to checking so that it cushions any possible overdraft, be sure to set up this option. If your bank doesn't have this possibility, shop around for a credit union or other bank that does offer this service. Beyond that, if your bank allows online access to your accounts, make sure you monitor your balance frequently so that you can avoid overdrafts altogether.

Few practices in life are smarter than always knowing the exact balance in your account. Make it a point to keep track of your balance, especially when it falls below $30 or $40. Knowledge is power—when you know how much money is in the bank, you know how to plan your spending more wisely.

Tithing and Giving

By common practice, many active churchgoers contribute a percentage of their income, often 10 percent, to their local church. Some people give based on a percentage of their gross income, others on their net pay. Regardless, the general concept is to donate the "firstfruits" of your labors, giving God an offering of gratitude before spending your paycheck on other things or in other categories.

Several single parents tell us that the discipline of "tithing," as it is called, is one of the most useful ways they have found for getting ahead financially.

"I know it doesn't seem to make much sense," one single dad remarks. "But when I give God the first 10 percent of my income every month, somehow the rest of my income goes further.

"I can't explain that to you, but I watch it happen every month. I'm not trying to sound all 'prosperity gospel' on you, but I have really found it true that when you tithe your income to God, things just work out better."

Other single parents make similar statements.

One single mother doesn't see it as supernatural, but as a practical reality.

"When I write my check to the church," she tells us, "that makes me more careful with what I have left. So my money lasts longer. I'm not sure whether it's a spiritual thing or it's just me being careful with the rest of my money.

"All I know is that when I tithe to God, my whole budget works out better. It's such a clear trend that I can't ignore it. It's just true."

Single parents often regret the fact that due to being poor, they can't give to charity or help those in need the way they wish they could. Yet other single parents actively choose to tithe on their income, or to make regular contributions to a church building fund or a missionary. These equally poor but regularly contributing single parents insist that their money seems to last longer and go further when they make regular giving a part of their budget.

Perhaps the best way to test these claims is to experiment with giving. Give a regular amount (percentage or dollar amount) on a steady basis and see if your financial tension eases or increases. The single parents we interviewed insist that regular giving not only feels great, it also produces a budget that is easier to manage and control. Some of them believe that "God blesses them" when they tithe. They believe this blessing occurs in financial realms.

Giving to a missionary, a charity, or a church can boost your self-esteem and make you feel like you are part of something larger than yourself. One of the most demeaning aspects of poverty is feeling unable to give. When you break out of that mind-set and begin to give regularly, you boost your self-confidence and increase your self-esteem.

While the purpose of giving is outside and beyond yourself, it is also true that as a giver, you receive tangible benefits by giving. One of those benefits, some single parents insist, is making progress toward your financial goals.

Life Insurance: The Luxury You Must Afford

The children of single parents are among the most vulnerable financially. They are particularly at risk if their sole custodial parent dies or is incapacitated by a serious illness.

Single parents know this, yet often remain uninsured, believing that they simply cannot afford to pay the premiums for needed coverage. Most single parents can clearly demonstrate that they are unable to pay for good insurance.

If you find it hard to ask for help from others, this category of help may be one of the simpler places to start. Asking your family members, close friends, or even your church for help with a life insurance premium may show you that, for the right cause or reason, people do stand ready to assist you.

"I told my dad I wanted to get some life insurance," one single mother reports. "I explained that if something happened to me, I wanted my kids to have a nest egg to fall back on.

"My dad saw that right away, and got excited about helping me. He ended up doing all the shopping online, getting rate quotes and comparisons. Then as we looked at everything, he told me that he would pay the premiums, at least for the first year.

"That was four years ago, and he's still paying the premiums. I can't tell you how much peace of mind it gives me to know that, if something happens to me, there is a sizeable insurance policy that will take care of my kids."

If you are employed, you may already be covered by a small level of life insurance through your company. Ask your supervisor or manager, the human resources department, or the owner of the business if you are already covered. You may discover that there is a $10,000 or $25,000 policy already in effect. It may also be possible to increase this coverage at an affordable price.

If you have an account at a credit union, you may have a similar small policy protecting you. Read the fine print on your account or ask a teller. If you're covered for $1000 or $2000 it may be possible to upgrade this coverage, and perhaps to have the premiums automatically deducted from your account.

> With a solid insurance policy in place, you'll feel better about yourself.

Your membership in professional organizations, a discount club, or other group may qualify you for life insurance at reduced rates. Your car insurance company may offer life insurance more cheaply because you are already a valued customer of one of their insurance lines. Ask questions and find out how much coverage is available, and at what cost.

Many of us avoid insurance salespersons because we do not like high-pressure selling tactics. If you personally know someone who works in the insurance field, consider whether you would be comfortable having a talk with this person about types of policies, amounts of coverage, and typical costs. Many people have an insurance agent in their family, among their neighbors, or within their congregation. Ask someone you know—your existing relationship with them may help you get friendly, objective, reasonable advice.

It is also possible to mostly or completely avoid agents by doing your shopping online. An online search for "life insurance" will turn up more Web sites than you could examine in a lifetime. Half a dozen of the major sites are easy to use—punch in a few key facts about yourself and quotes pop up immediately.*

No one likes to think about death or dying. Yet if you are a single parent it is wise to think about your children and realize that if you don't provide for them, their future may be uncertain at best. One way to wisely protect your children is by having an adequate amount of life insurance in force at all times.

With or without help from others, take a good look at obtaining at least a small amount of coverage. Prices for life insurance tend to be lower at younger ages, so it may be to your advantage to obtain coverage now while you are young and in good health. Putting off coverage until later may be a costly decision to make.

With a solid insurance policy in place, you'll feel better about yourself. You'll realize that you've made a wise choice to protect your children if the unthinkable should happen while they're still in your care.

■ ■ ■ ■

The ideas we've mentioned on the previous pages are huge basic steps that will take you a long way toward developing more financial margin in your life. There are many other good ideas out there; after putting the basics in place, we urge you to creatively explore other thoughts and possibilities.

One place to start is the "Resources" at the back of this book. There you will find listed several organizations that specialize in helping you make and keep to a workable financial plan for your family.

As you enjoy more financial stability bit by bit, you'll find that your confidence in managing your money will spread to your children. Not only will they start feeling more secure and confident, but you'll be giving them basic training toward managing their own money some day.

---

* Two major sites are Insure.com and Quotesmith.com—both of these sites are user-friendly and can show you quickly how much a policy would cost.

12

Dating and Relationships

How the Choices You Make
May Affect Your Children

■ ■ ■ ■

I decided to remain single while my girls
were growing up, and think about dating later.
Now that my girls are grown I've gotten pretty used
to being alone, but now I'm finally open to thinking
about a new relationship.

MADELYN, SINGLE MOTHER

Single parents—both mothers and fathers—tend to receive more advice about dating than about any other topic. Wouldn't it be nice if all your "helpers" would simply give money instead of sharing their advice with you? But instead of helping in tangible financial ways, many friends and family members want to "help you out" by making sure that someone is taking you out—on dates. They believe that if they can only find "the man for you" or connect you with "the right woman" then somehow your life will be magically transformed into a place of delight and joy.*

Your friends and family have good intentions—probably— but their dating advice is seldom useful, and may even be a highly negative distraction for you as you mature, grow, and learn the skills you'll need for the road ahead.

---

* If you are a single mother thinking about marrying again, you may want to skip ahead to "Living It Out." In it, we interview a single mother who made that same choice—she decided to remarry. We've included the high-lights of her honest, candid, and extremely open remarks about daily life in a real remarriage. Her comments may be the most helpful words we've ever heard, firsthand, from a person who is living in a remarriage.

Far too many single parents attempt to escape the pressures of single life by rushing into a remarriage. Stressed out by poverty, struggling to cope with out-of-control children, seeming to have a complete lack of positive future prospects, single parents are vulnerable to the belief that a new marriage will solve or erase most of their problems, making their lives better.

As they soon discover, it simply isn't so. If you are living in poverty before a remarriage, you will most likely have financial stress afterward. If your children do not behave well before you marry again, they will probably keep on not behaving well after your new union. They may in fact behave worse.

Nearly three out of four remarriages are ending within the first decade, most of these within the first five years. The "failure rate" of remarriages ranges from 20 to 33 percent higher than the same rate for original marriages. So if original marriages are ending at a high rate—and they are—remarriages are ending at a rate that is even higher.

In California right now—late 2006—two out of three remarriages are ending within the first 24 months. The primary stated reason for the breakup of these marriages is a major difference in the attitude and approach about raising children and the discipline of those children within the home. In other words, the children of previous relationships tend to be a big factor in the success or failure of new relationships. A couple remarries with the best of intentions, but soon discovers that each person manages children in radically different ways. We'll explore these difficulties later in this chapter.

For now, what is important for you to learn is that the odds against having a successful and lasting remarriage are dizzyingly high. Most remarriages simply do not thrive. They do not go the distance. They do not endure.*

In Western culture, relationships have taken on a disposable

---

* Against this dismal backdrop we've written *Happily Remarried*—a book about the best practices and healthy habits of successful remarried couples. If you are thinking about remarriage, please consider reading *Happily Remarried* during your dating and courtship. The book will show you, through examples that are both positive and negative, how to approach many of your new challenges. The couples we interviewed for the book were honest about their mistakes and their failures, yet they also showed us the successful strategies they use for blending families, managing money, and raising well-adjusted children   .

We wrote *Happily Remarried* in a genuine attempt to help remarried couples find lasting commitment within their current relationships. It is a massive chal-lenge to undertake. As we mentioned previously, more than two million adults get divorced each year in the United States, many of them for a second time or beyond.

nature. There is a tangible sense that if a current relationship isn't working, the solution is to end it, move out, start over, and try again. We have interviewed persons who were in a fourth or fifth marriage—and often this current marriage was also in trouble.

Many single parents begin dating with the idea that remarriage is an attractive and viable option. Even though they've lived through the end of a previous relationship, they somehow manage to believe that the next union can be different. After all, wasn't the ex-partner the source of most of the problems? Since that person is out of the picture, the future looks bright and filled with hope.

Let's be blunt for a moment: Many people get married for the first time before they have grown up as persons. A significant number of original marriages include at least one partner who is immature and unprepared to make a lifelong commitment to another person.

This is also true of remarriages. The trauma of a marriage ending provides a man or woman with a wonderful opportunity to grow, mature, and become wise. Yet far too many divorced persons rush right back into the dating life, hoping to find a new relationship that will become a marriage and thus acquire permanence. Instead of learning life's difficult lessons and becoming wiser, these hasty single parents may look for happiness in all the wrong places—usually in the arms (or perhaps the bed) of someone else who has not yet matured into wise adulthood.

Rushing into a new relationship is a prescription for failure. If there is a new relationship in your future, and perhaps there is, you will do well to slow down, learn the lessons of this season in your life, and face forward with a mature understanding of who you are as a person and what kind of partner would be compatible with you for the long term. If you hurry up and get remarried, you may find that your next divorce arrives just as quickly.

Children and Remarriage

As children adjust to the trauma of a separation or divorce, they gradually begin to develop a sense of what their new life and new family circle will be like.

They often bounce back and forth between two different houses, having a few clothing and personal items in Dad's house in addition to their primary life and their major collection of clothing at Mom's home. It takes time to make this transition. Children need every moment of that time to adjust and cope.

As a single parent, you may have primary physical custody of your children. If so, you will become the leader of a new family unit that differs in character from the former one. Your children will adjust to this new way of life. They'll adapt to your moods, preferences, and boundaries. Although the road to serenity may be marked with potholes and speed bumps, children do tend to adjust to new situations, particularly if there is the continuity of having the same mother as always, or the same dad as before, in the new situation.

As they make these adjustments, children of single parents tend to resist their parents' desires to date. If the dating progresses to a desire for permanence, children can find this idea very threatening to their sense of well-being. When a remarriage occurs, this new union upsets the fragile balance of the children's worldview and understanding. Older children may become greatly distressed at the prospect of their mother or father marrying again—even if their other parent has left the family and begun a new relationship.

In part, this is because many children of divorce cling to the hope that their birth mother and father will reunite someday. This idealistic dream may survive childhood and be present in adult children of divorce who, against all odds, continue to wish that their parents would not only get along and be nice to each other, but would return to each other as life partners, reconnecting the original marriage union.

Remarriage tends to shatter this dream within a child, and thus can be a threatening and highly opposed event. Before a child can learn to be genuinely happy for you as you form a new relationship, that child first must learn to be unselfish in his or her focus. Generally speaking, children do not move toward unselfishness until adolescence or beyond—if ever.

We interviewed a single father whose teen daughter wanted him to start dating again. Exploring her thoughts and feelings, we learned that her primary motivator was that her dad "was lonely all the time." Having acquired an unselfish mind-set, this adolescent girl wanted to see a smile on her father's face. She wanted to see him relax, play his guitar, sing, and "be crazy" more often. Watching her father cope with loneliness as a single parent, this teen daughter wanted the best for him—in her view, a new woman in his life.

This kind of unselfishness is rare among the children of single parents. Younger children want to keep Mom all to themselves or cling to Dad forever. They are not willing to allow their mother or father to share affection with a new adult: The transaction seems to involve too much "losing" for the children. A child may wonder, *If my mom loves a new man, will she still love me?*

Reasons to Consider Remaining Single

Some of the wisest single parents we interviewed for this project spoke eloquently about their choice to remain single while their children were young. Several of the mothers wept briefly while describing their own loneliness and pain, yet even though sad, they were not willing to date or seek companionship. Putting the needs of their children ahead of their own, these women decided that the children's well-being would be better served by a mother who remained single, focusing all of her attention and affection on her kids.

This was not a recommendation flowing from us as family counselors in the direction of these single parents. Rather, the roles were reversed—we were seeking the wisdom of single parents, asking them what advice they had for others about dating and remarriage while raising children after a divorce. As we gained and received this wisdom from our interview subjects, their reasons for not dating and remarrying fell into three general categories.

1. Putting the Children First

Many single parents, especially single mothers, believe that giving their children their entire undivided focus is the best way to help the children cope with the suffering and loss that followed the breakup of the original family. These parents express the belief that dating would probably be a distraction for them, rather than a form of help.

"My kids have to come first," one single mother exclaimed as we talked. "They know that's true because I've told them over and over since the divorce. If I was out dating again, my focus would be on a new guy and how my relationship was going, not on my kids and how they are doing.

"I can't go two directions at once," this mom insisted. "Either I can really be here for my children and help them get through this, or I can be out there dating around and meeting guys, always wondering if a relationship has a future. For me, that's distracting. I want to keep my focus on my kids. They need me."

Other single mothers made similar comments.

"I'm going to get them through high school before I even think about dating again," one apparently successful single mom stated. "I don't let myself get interested in anyone; I stay busy with my job and busy raising my kids. If there's a man in my future, that's exactly where he is—in my future."

At least one single father had the same perspective, echoing almost verbatim the same comment we'd heard from a single mom. "My kids come first," this dad explained to us over cappuccinos as his two young children played nearby. "Whatever is best for them, that's what I'm going to do. And frankly I don't think my dating around or looking for a new wife is what's best for them—at least not while they're so young. I'll deal with that later."

While consensus among the experts is rare, a growing body of evidence suggests that kids are much more able to cope with having a single-parent family than they are with the challenge of being "blended" into a stepfamily. Experts are beginning to respectfully suggest that single parents consider remaining single, so that the children do not undergo the stresses of interacting with new siblings, a parent's new partner, or both.

Regardless of the experts' views, we heard this theme expressed by wise, mature single parents whom we interviewed. Lonely, stressed, and often feeling like they were failing, these single moms and dads told us they were choosing to focus on the children and their needs, rather than on their personal emotional or relational happiness.

2. Waiting for the Original Partner to Return

We spoke with several single parents whose choice to remain single was a theological or spiritual one. They believed that remarriage was not a wise choice for themselves under any

> The meaning of freedom certainly includes a choice to remain single and await a possible reconciliation with one's original partner.

circumstances. Instead, they viewed it as their role to wait patiently for the potential return of their former partner. In some cases, these single moms and dads admitted that their absentee partners had already remarried.

One single father was adamant about this issue, stating that he would not remarry at any time for any reason. This lonely dad believed that God would be pleased if he waited on the potential, eventual future return of his ex-wife, who had already married a second time, divorced a second time, and was living with a new unmarried partner as we conducted the interview.

"I will wait for her forever," he told us. He also admitted in a candid and far-ranging conversation that he was lonely most of the time, frequently jealous of married and remarried couples even among his closest friends. "I'm sorry I feel that way, but I do," he confessed quietly. "It's not like I'd rather be lonely."

We have enormous respect for single parents who make this choice. In our own reading of the relevant scriptures, particularly 1 Corinthians 7:10-17, we see biblical freedom for a postdivorce believer whose partner does not wish to return to the original marriage. "In such cases the Christian partner, whether husband or wife, is free to act" (1 Corinthians 7:15). Yet the meaning of freedom certainly includes a choice to remain single and await a possible reconciliation with one's original partner. To express one's freedom in this way is admirable. We have encountered a number of single parents who do not intend to ever seek another partner, because they are waiting for their first partner to return.

3. Keeping Life Less Complicated

The third general category of response centered around a desire to keep life less complicated. Relationships can confuse, challenge, and absorb us as we explore them and consider forming a permanent union. Some single parents told us they were staying away from dating because they "didn't want the hassle" of sorting out romantic possibilities while they were trying to recover from a messy divorce.

Those who spoke in this way were concerned about their children, yet it was not the kids' confusion that was being avoided. Rather, these adults knew themselves well enough to know that trying to date and sort out one's feelings can become immensely distracting. It is possible to waste enormous amounts of time and energy reading the signs, probing for someone else's true thoughts, and wading through the kind of trauma that many of us remember from high school.

"I can't take that right now," said one single mother. "I've got enough confusion and uncertainty. I don't need another whole category of things that I'm confused about and trying to sort out."

These three categories formed the primary groupings into which responses fell among single parents choosing not to date or remarry. Some of those who responded in this category left their options open for the future, insisting simply that they weren't ready to consider dating "right now" or "for a while." Others told us that their choice was either permanent or lifelong, or would at least endure for as long as they had children living under their roof.

"Maybe later," said one single mom in her 30s. "Maybe when the house is empty. Maybe after my kids get married." Her response typifies many who told us that for as long as children were in their direct care, dating and remarriage were not going to be considered.

There are wise and intelligent reasons to consider postponing your own hopes for enduring romance while school-age children live in your home. You may be able to give them stability and a sense of permanence that will greatly help them recover from the trauma and difficulty of divorce. Although you are only one person, it is also true that you are a person to whom your children look for moral and emotional guidance. Your choices affect how your children view the world around them, and also how they see themselves.

Why Some People Recommend New Relationships

We can also report that we interviewed quite a few single parents who actively hoped to remarry. Meanwhile, they were definitely open to dating: Some of them were involved in serious relationships. Most of these reported to us that they were "taking it slow" because of having had such a bad experience in their prior unions.

We inquired about how the process of dating was affecting the family dynamics in the homes of these single parents. Responses varied, but tended to fall into one of two broad categories among those who dated or were actively considering a remarriage.

Listed below are the two primary reasons we heard from single parents as they discussed their motivation for dating and seeking a new life partner.

1. We Are Not Meant to Be Alone

This response typified the single fathers who were among this group of respondents. Their view, frequently expressed with passion and eloquence, was that while functioning as a single they "lacked balance" in their lives. Only by participating in a meaningful relationship could these persons achieve the kind of inner peace and personal balance they valued.

One dad is typical in his comments.

"Left to myself I am too driven, too intense, and too much of a perfectionist—and I always have been. I know that about myself—I also know when I'm involved in a fairly deep relationship, I tend to slow down, relax more often, and 'smell the roses' while living my life.

"Frankly, I don't do those things when I'm just on my own. I am literally a different person when I'm in a relationship. I'm more stable, more settled, more slow to anger. I'm calmer when I'm with someone."

Directly or indirectly, this father views the existence of a dating relationship as being a benefit to his children—because it tends to produce a father in the house who is a more balanced single parent and generally a happier and more relaxed presence. Whether this is a way of rationalizing a romance or whether this accurately describes a useful prescription for type A personalities, this single father assures us that dating is the pathway to peaceful living.

Several single mothers felt this way as well. They described themselves as "out of balance" or "needing someone else to keep me focused" when living a life that was entirely single. Although raising their kids alone, these moms told us that having an active dating life was a way of keeping their perspective, helping them be more productive and stable as parents to their growing children.

Mothers invoked the well-being of their children also.

"I'm crazy without a man in my life," sighed one single mother. "I need someone else to keep me together. I'm sure my kids can see that. Everyone who knows me can probably see that!"

Respondents in this category assured us that dating was not a distraction, but that the existence of a meaningful or potentially meaningful relationship brought stability, balance, depth, and perspective into lives that needed these gifts. If true, it seems likely that the children would indeed benefit, despite their probable sense of "loss" at losing their parent to an adult relationship.

2. Showing Kids Another View of Family Life

A large group of the respondents in this category told us that, having "failed" in a marriage (their term), they were ready to show their children what a healthy and loving marriage looked like.

Several single parents we interviewed were nominally Christian or not yet Christian during their marriages. Having found a personal relationship with God since the divorce or perhaps because of it, these single parents now wanted to enter a "godly marriage" and thus show their children a Christian example.

"I lived with my first husband for a few years before we got married," one single mother shared. "Honestly, our years of living together were better than our years of being married. Once we got married, he started treating me a lot worse, or at least it felt that way to me."

When the marriage ended, the suddenly single mom returned to her parents' home and, with it, her parents' church. She reconnected with faith and began trying to live by Christian principles. She comments on how this affects her current relationships: "When I started dating Dan, I told him right away that I didn't believe in sex outside of marriage," this single mom asserts. "He laughed and told me he didn't believe in that either. So we are already starting this relationship in a lot better way than I started my marriage."

Another single mother told us that her children had seen nothing but fighting and arguing in her first marriage. She explained that she hoped to remarry someday (she is dating someone now, but still early in the relationship) because she wants to show her young children how a husband and wife are supposed to treat each other.

"Greg drank a lot," this mother explained to us. "And although I wasn't drinking, the fighting was my fault too. He would get drunk and start yelling at me, and I would yell right back at him. I wasn't going to put up with that!"

Seated inside a church classroom, this single parent tells us that she's learned a lot about how to control her anger, in part through seminars that her local church sponsored and conducted. She is confident that, if she does remarry in the future, her life as a wife will not be characterized by the kinds of violent verbal outbursts of which she was guilty before.

Single parents in this group assured us that setting a new, better example for their children was a high priority for them. They told us that they wanted to remarry so the children could live in a loving home, with a mother and father who loved God and each other.

"Otherwise," said one single dad, "they'll never actually see what a loving marriage and a godly home are supposed to look like."

Whatever Your Choice, the Right Speed Is *Slow*

We are frequently interviewed by broadcast or print journalists who ask us to explain why so many marriages fail. As we've discussed in the pages of this book, marriages often occur between two people who may be chronological adults, but who are far from being adults in their emotional lives. Many people who get married are simply too immature and too self-centered to succeed in making and keeping a lifelong commitment to another person.

This same phenomenon affects remarriages as well. When a person suffers through the trauma of a marriage ending, she may regress to a prior emotional state. Although mature while married, the trauma of divorce may set her back a few years in emotional stability. When a man is abandoned by his wife, he may find himself reverting to adolescent behaviors and childish attitudes. Although he may have been "the mature one" in his original marriage, divorce pushes him back into a previous emotional life he thought he'd put well behind him.

Remarriages can thus be places where one or both of the parties are immature or emotionally unstable. This reality limits the prospects for a healthy and thriving remarriage; it may also partially explain the high rate of failure among remarried unions.

There is no substitute for taking it slow after you've been divorced. As we wrote our book *Moving Forward After Divorce,* we heard this theme continually from divorced persons who had found healing and maturity after crisis and change knocked them off balance.

"I'm not in a hurry," one divorced woman shared with us as she considered the prospect of remarriage. "I've learned a lot about myself. I've realized I've got some growing up to do. I think I'd like to do my growing up first, then maybe get married later on."

Her perspective abounds in wisdom. When you allow the trauma of divorce or abandonment to help you grow up, you bless and benefit any potential future life partner by becoming a more stable, more mature, more self-aware person. Remarriages are challenging enough without attempting them while immature or emotionally needy. Taking the time to find balance and peace is a great way to prepare yourself for a future life partner.

The proper speed for moving ahead is—*slow*.

If in the aftermath of a divorce you feel like you'll never want to be in a relationship again, at any time or for any reason, be slow to share this feeling with those around you. Your statement might come back to haunt you: If you end up pursuing a relationship a few years later, people may say, "But I thought you were through with all of that!"

If in the aftermath of a messy divorce you feel like a new relationship is exactly the cure that you need, please be assured it isn't. New relationships are places in which we repeat our mistakes from previous relationships—unless we have grown, matured, and made progress after reflecting on the lessons of the previous union.

As a single parent, be wary of other singles who define their past problems as being the fault of "my ex." While it is natural and logical to assign blame to others, one hallmark of emerging maturity is the ability to say, "The end of the marriage was probably my fault too." Except in the most extreme cases, it will usually be true that both parties made mistakes in a relationship, and that these mistakes may have been a factor in the end of the marriage. Instead of blaming others for every negative outcome that occurs, mature persons look in the mirror and figure out how they can become better partners in a future relationship.

It takes time to become a mature person.

Instead of rushing to declare yourself a lifelong single, instead of hurrying into the dating scene in order to find a new partner, slow down and learn the lessons of the season that you're living in. Get to know your children more deeply and more fully than you've ever had the chance to do before. Get to know yourself: Find out how others view you and learn from those perspectives. Learn more about God, discover more about relationships, and resolve to be a new person in the future, whether alone or in a marriage.

■■■■

As family counselors, we do not have a one-size-fits-all approach to the question of dating and remarriage for divorced persons. We deeply respect those singles who believe that God's best for them is to remain single, awaiting the possible future return of a former partner. We also respect those who explore their biblical freedom by forming new unions. We know dozens of remarried couples whose marriages exemplify the very best qualities of godly marriage and Christian adulthood. These remarriages are miles ahead of many of the original marriages we know. So in other words, the fact that a relationship is a second or third attempt at marriage in no way limits the ability of a union to exemplify godly principles and Christian ideals.

Again, the closest thing we have to general advice is, *Go slowly.*

You will receive much advice from others, most of it unsolicited. You will receive theological advice, spiritual advice, social advice, and every other kind of counsel and input. Listen politely but stand firm: Do not jump to conclusions. When you do get ready to move ahead, do so after carefully and prayerfully considering your children and their needs. When you do get ready to move ahead, do so with a wise awareness of your own gifts and limitations.

We know lifelong singles, including single parents, who are balanced and whole as persons, lacking nothing in order to have a good and fulfilling life.

We know remarried persons, including former single parents, who have formed unions that we greatly admire: filled with unselfish love and abiding commitment.

Regardless of the direction you choose, do so without haste.

Your children will watch a wise process unfold, because they'll see it being led by a wise person: you. Build your self-respect and gain the respect of others by moving forward with dignity and grace.

Living It Out

Learning from One Single Parent's Experience

■ ■ ■ ■

GINNY GETS REMARRIED

In this chapter we interview a single parent who has chosen to get remarried. During the course of our interview session, she is extremely candid about how that choice has affected her life. In the pages of this chapter, you'll meet a remarkable person who is adjusting to life after singleness.

■ ■ ■ ■

Virginia meets us for coffee at a busy spot in a fast-growing suburb of Phoenix, Arizona. She arrives for our appointment 15 minutes early. We join a line of nearly a dozen people waiting to approach the cashier.

"Call me Ginny," she smiles, glancing at her watch. "I've got 90 minutes or so today, and if we don't get finished, I'm sure I could meet you again later."

We chat about children and families as we await our turn to order. The coffee shop is busy today. Despite the desert heat a steady line of customers opens the door and joins our queue along the bakery counter.

"My two are 14 and 11 now," Ginny sighs. "They're both growing up so fast! Elizabeth—she's the oldest—is already hyperbusy with soccer and choir and her youth group at church. David is in his first year of middle school, and so far it's not going very well for him. He's smaller than other boys his age…"

> "He looked at me and said, 'So, is it okay?' and for a few minutes I didn't realize what he meant."

A few minutes later we sip frozen coffee drinks on an outdoor terrace, shaded from the blazing sun by a roof extension. The misters dispense bursts of spray a few feet above our table, cooling the air nicely. We need the help—the outdoor temperature is well over a hundred degrees.

"Where should I start?" Ginny wonders as we settle in for the interview. "What kind of things are you interested in?"

"Let's begin with the divorce—before if you want," Lisa suggests.

Ginny pauses to gather her thoughts.

"Okay," she agrees. "One of my best friends told me she knew for certain that my husband was having an affair. I didn't believe her at first, though I couldn't see any reason why she would make up something like that! So I listened to her and kept listening. It all turned out to be true. Kevin was sleeping with a mutual friend of ours. It had been going on for about three months before I found out.

"I confronted him about it, and he admitted it. He told me he'd been thinking about asking me for a divorce. He told me he was glad I knew: Now it made things easier for him."

Ginny stops for a moment, gathering her thoughts.

"I was in shock. I thought we had a pretty normal marriage. We had two kids, and there'd been some stress from having two young children in the house, just normal stuff. Maybe Kevin and I weren't as close as we had been, but I really thought everything was okay.

"I was busy trying to be a wife and mother, adjusting to the changes in my schedule and routine, struggling to take the weight off after each pregnancy. I wasn't working—the kids were too young—but I kept the house up and things were going pretty good for us. I wasn't head over heels in love anymore, but I thought Kevin and I had a solid, loving relationship going. I thought our marriage was pretty good. We went to church, and we had friends there…"

Was it her husband's idea to end their marriage? Was it Kevin who first brought up this possibility? Did he ask her for a divorce?

"He did," Ginny recalls. "And it was just like that—he asked me. He looked at me and said, 'So, is it okay?' and for a few minutes I didn't realize what he meant. Then I figured out that he was asking me if it was 'okay' if he moved in with Tina, if he abandoned me and the kids, if he filed for a divorce…

"What do you say to that? I just sat there, not really believing what I was hearing. Later I kept thinking of a lot of really smart things I should have said back to him. Things like 'No, it is certainly *not* okay!' would have been good. But I just sat there. I was kind of frozen and in shock."

Kevin eventually asked the question directly: If he filed for a divorce, how would his wife respond? Would they have to fight about everything, or could they agree to make some decisions about money, custody of the kids, and other issues?

"I still didn't know what to tell him," Ginny recounts. "I told him I needed some time—*that* was an understatement—then I went outside, sat on the back porch, and had a good long cry."

■■■■

With the help of a few good friends from her church, Ginny decided not to oppose the divorce, although she strongly wanted to stay married. Instead of denying her husband his freedom, she focused on trying to get the best possible deal in terms of caring for her children and her financial future. It was hard for her; she disagrees with the idea of divorce, believing that marriage is forever. Her friends helped her focus on the business and financial aspects of ending a marriage.

She was mostly satisfied with the economic outcome.

"We didn't have any money," she admits. "So it wasn't like I was trying to hold on to our wealth. What wealth? We hadn't been married long—about eight years at that time—and we were struggling financially. So the divorce was more about what was going to happen to the house, who was going to pay which bills, and things like that. We weren't fighting over some family fortune."

Ginny received primary physical custody of the children (no argument from Kevin) and also kept the house, although she had no idea how she was going to pay for it. Kevin was happy to keep his nearly new SUV, allowing his wife to retain the small equity they had acquired in their home.

"After I got a job, I refinanced the house and got smaller payments," Ginny says. "That may not have been the smartest thing to do, but I needed to save some money every month. Getting a lower mortgage payment really helped."

We ask her about getting a job.

"I had no skills," is Ginny's assessment. "A friend of mine offered to help me write up a résumé—but there was nothing to put in it! I hadn't worked since I got married. I didn't even know how to look for a job."

How did she find employment?

"Well, obviously everyone in the world knew about the divorce," Ginny recalls, "and people kept asking me how they could help. So I would say the same thing to everyone that asked me: 'Do you happen to know where I could find a decent job?'"

Her method worked. A friend of her father's knew of an opening at his company. The role? Office assistant, day hours, full-time, with benefits including good health insurance. Ginny applied for the job, but without much hope of actually being selected.

"I think Richard pulled some strings." Ginny smiles. "He and my dad are real close friends. My parents were so upset about the divorce, and they really wanted to help out, but they weren't in a place, financially, to do much to help me. So I think my dad asked Richard to make it happen, and maybe Richard had some influence."

■ ■ ■ ■

Ginny went to work, which meant someone needed to care for her two kids.

"I got Elizabeth into a pre-K program," Ginny tells us. "It was an experimental, all-day program instead of the usual half-day kind.

So that really helped, though Lizzy got done with school two hours before my work day ended, so I still needed help with picking her up.

"David was two. I found a day-care center near Lizzy's school. It was way too expensive, but what could I do? They took David all day, so he didn't need to be picked up until after I was done with work.

"My mom was the one who picked up Elizabeth every day after school. She would drive over to the school, pick up Lizzy, take her to my house, and stay there with her until David and I got home from work.

"I remember my mom telling me once, 'I'm so glad I don't have David for two hours before you get home!' And we both laughed. David was two—he was really out of control in those years. He was a handful."

How does Ginny remember those years when she thinks about them?

"I was going crazy. I was working at a real job for the first time in my life, trying to keep it together at work. Then I was coming home to two little kids whose daddy had left them, and who hadn't seen me all day.

"I loved those kids, but they were just so demanding! They would cling to me and follow me around and stick to me like glue. I couldn't get anything done in the evenings because my kids were crawling all over me."

How did she respond to the pressure and the challenges?

Ginny smiles at the question. "I started dating!" she exclaims. "Isn't that what you'd recommend?"

We laugh together as the misters whoosh overhead.

"I think I needed to prove to myself that I was still attractive, that I could still get a man to look at me and ask me out, I don't know," Ginny muses. "I had my first date about three months after Kevin filed for the divorce. Kevin was gone, I was lonely, it felt okay to date even though I wasn't legally 'free' yet."

Did the dating work out? Did Ginny gain the approval she needed?

"I met some interesting guys," she says wryly. "I mean, they were nice, all of them. A lot of them were divorced, just like me. We'd go out a few times, we'd start to get close—and then I'd realize, *Do I really want to spend the rest of my life with this guy?*

"I did a lot of short-term dating. Three or four times with the same guy, then I would kind of lose interest. I had one guy that I liked for about six months, and that was nice, but in the end it was just the same: I couldn't imagine being married to him for the rest of my life. I just couldn't see that."

■■■■

What changed, and when? What was the pathway to remarriage?

"I met a guy at work," Ginny says slowly. "I wasn't flirting with him, I didn't think of him in that way. He was older, almost old enough to be my dad. He was very professional, he dressed really nice, he always treated me well.

"Around the office or in the lunchroom, when I would talk to him he just always seemed to respect me. I hadn't experienced that; I hadn't been respected on the job, as a professional person, as a career woman. So I found myself kind of gravitating to him, not even realizing it."

How did the relationship develop? When did it begin to change?

"Well, he heard my whole life story," Ginny says with a rueful grin. "After I got to know him, I felt really comfortable telling him what was going on. He was a patient listener—he had to hear all about my kids. By then both Lizzy and David were in school; David was usually getting into some kind of trouble. I would sit there and just talk about everything that was going on in my life, mostly my kids, and Jim would just listen to me.

"I told him about my marriage to Kevin, about how it ended, about how lonely I was and how pointless the whole dating scene was. It never even crossed my mind that I was saying these things to someone I might have a relationship with—"

Ginny interrupts her narrative.

"It really never did," she realizes. "I wasn't self-conscious at all. I could just talk to him about anything, and he'd listen to me. I never felt like I was being inspected or evaluated or judged.

"One morning I was talking to him at coffee break and he looked at me. He kind of said, 'Why don't we go *out* for lunch today?' and he smiled. I said, 'Sure,' without even thinking about it—not realizing it was kind of, sort of, a date.

"Instead of talking with me in the lunchroom he drove me to Chili's. He insisted on paying for both of us. It was a little awkward at first—like when he said, 'Table for two,' and I felt like we were a couple for the first time. But after that our conversation was just completely normal, except we could talk more freely because we were out of the office.

"I guess that was our first 'date,' but it wasn't romantic. We just had the same kind of conversation we always had, except we were eating better, and it was just the two of us, and we were away from the stress of the office.

"We got back to the office and as we were walking in the door, he said, 'We should do this more often,' and I said, 'That would be great!' I guess that's how we started dating, although even then I didn't think we were really dating."

■ ■ ■ ■

A nearby table turns noisy and we pause for a while. When the noise dies down a bit, we continue our interview.

When did she know the relationship was turning romantic?

Ginny smiles.

"It was probably our third or fourth lunch out of the office," she recalls. "He looked at me and said, 'You know, we could do this on a weekend sometime,' and that's when I got it. We were actually dating! I laughed and told him I'd love to go out with him on a weekend, but we'd have to figure out what to do with Elizabeth and David.

"He looked right at me and said, 'Bring them along!' and he meant it."

The couple's first official date was a foursome: Ginny, her two kids, and Jim, a single man who had never married. They went to a Disney movie; then out for ice cream. Jim paid for everything.

"It went pretty well," Ginny admits. "David was his usual self; he made a lot of noise in the theater and wasn't always on his best behavior. Lizzy did really well. She was quiet during the movie, and she liked Jim the moment she met him."

The foursome began getting together every weekend for a meal, a movie, or some kind of event. Jim took the group to a baseball game; another time he took them to a water park, which the kids thoroughly enjoyed. As time passed, the four grew comfortable being together. By the time Ginny realized that she and Jim were officially dating, her defenses were lowered somewhat. She was not resisting or avoiding close relationships as intensely as she had before.

"When I finally got to the stage where I would stop and think about being married to a guy for the rest of my life—I could see it happening," Ginny recalls. "Thinking about being with Jim all my life felt comfortable and easy. It didn't stress me out to think about marriage. I was thinking about it for a long time before it came up."

How did Jim propose to her?

"It was really sweet," Ginny tells us. "We weren't really doing much as just the two of us, except we went to lunch more often while we were at work. Most of the time on weekends if we were together, it was all four of us, not the two of us.

"One weekend Jim told me he'd arranged for my parents to watch Lizzy and David on Saturday night, so that we could go out by ourselves. I remember thinking it was really thoughtful of him, but that's all I thought. I didn't suspect that he was going to propose to me. I really didn't see it coming.

"We went to dinner at a nice Italian place, amazing food, and we were almost done with the meal when Jim got kind of nervous. I could tell something was up—he got a worried look on his face. I hadn't seen him like that.

"He took my hand, and he looked directly at me, and he said something like 'I know you could do a lot better—you're a beautiful and attractive woman—but if you'd be willing to put up with me, I'd be honored to be your husband.'

"I just looked at him. I didn't know what to say. Then I almost started to cry, but I caught myself. I looked at him again and said 'Yes!' and he got the biggest smile on his face. I thought he was going to burst!

"That's when I *did* cry. I just cried and cried, going on forever, and Jim probably wanted to change his mind. But I was so happy I just wept. I think the waiters were probably kind of worried about us."

■ ■ ■ ■

Ginny and Jim picked out rings together, mutually agreeing that it was silly to spend a fortune on jewelry. Why not put that money into a college fund for Elizabeth and David, or something practical like that?

We ask her about premarriage counseling.

"We really didn't have any. We had started going to church together as the four of us—to Jim's church—and we asked one of the pastors there if he would marry us. We had one appointment with him, he asked us a few basic questions, and then he recommended a book he thought we should read together during our devotional time. That was about it."

The couple's official courtship was brief. Once they decided to marry, neither of them saw any good reason to wait. Besides, the news was sure to circulate at the office: It seemed simpler and wiser to get married as soon as possible rather than deal with endless gossip or teasing at work.

Their choice of housing? Jim's place, which was larger than the home Ginny had been living in with her children. It had the additional advantage of being completely paid for. Jim, a thrifty bachelor for many years, had prepaid his mortgage and owned the home free and clear.

Perhaps the only negative of the move was a change of schools for Ginny's children, who were both in the same elementary school.

Aware of this potential issue, the new couple agreed to leave the kids in their existing school for the remainder of the current school year, even though it meant extra driving time on a daily basis for several months.

"Changing schools was probably good for David," Ginny says today. "Before that he was in trouble all the time at school, even when he was little. I think starting over in a new place might have been good for him. Lizzy didn't seem too upset about it—she really liked Jim and she really liked his big house. Lizzy was the one of us who seemed the most excited about the whole process—my getting married again, us moving in with Jim.

"We planned a wedding that involved both of my kids—Lizzy as a flower girl, David as the ring bearer—and of course David's part turned into a complete disaster. But the wedding was nice: We did it cheaply at our church and invited some friends from the office and a few other friends and relatives.

"It was really low-key. We weren't interested in wasting money on some big production. We had a friend cater the reception so we saved money on that. We sat around one of the fellowship rooms in the church enjoying Mexican food and eating lots and *lots* of ice cream and cake."

For Ginny, one of the biggest advantages of getting remarried arrived a few months later.

"I got to quit my job." She smiles. "I didn't resent working, I really didn't. I liked getting a paycheck and putting it in the bank. I liked the sense of accomplishment I got from earning money and taking care of my kids. But wow—it was wonderful when I got to give notice at work. I couldn't believe it! After almost four years of steadily working, I got to return to my role as a full-time homemaker, wife, and mother of two kids.

"It felt *so great* to give notice, quit commuting, and stay home!"

■ ■ ■ ■

Gradually our discussion turns to daily life in a remarriage. What is working well, what isn't working so well, what things have turned out differently than she might have expected?

Ginny is thoughtful and extremely candid in her responses.

"Life with Kevin was exciting in a way," she remarks. "He was crazy and fun, probably because he was also so immature. When it was good with Kevin, it was really good. I would have stayed with him forever, even after he cheated. Of course, I wouldn't have stayed with him if he kept on cheating—and he probably would have."

> "Living alone was about trying to pay bills, chasing around after my kids, and dating guys I knew were too unstable or uninteresting to be with for life."

Ginny looks off across the parking lot for a while.

"I wouldn't say life with Jim is extremely exciting." She chooses her words very carefully. "He is loving and attentive and kind. He is a complete gentleman. He's great with the kids—much more patient with David than I am. Lizzy absolutely adores him. We have a settled, stable family life that I never had with Kevin—that probably I never would have had with Kevin.

"But *exciting* is not a word that applies to my life right now. Maybe I'm beyond that stage, or at least I should be. I do know that I wouldn't trade what I've got right now for any kind of 'excitement'—I'd be giving up too much. So maybe I'm the one who has changed: I'm looking for different things now, I'm at a different place in my life.

"Jim is older than I am, and I notice that sometimes. We laugh at different kinds of humor, or he makes a reference to something I don't understand. He grew up in a different generation than I did, and I'm noticing our differences more now than I did while we were just friends.

"Does this sound like I'm unhappy? Don't worry, I'm not. Does this sound like I'm dissatisfied? I'm not that, either. It's more like…"

Here Ginny pauses again, trying to find words to express herself.

"I just want to give people an accurate picture of remarriage, or at least of the kind of remarriage I'm in," she continues. "I am married to a faithful, stable, loving man who treats me wonderfully. He is a great father to my children, and now they're really 'his' children too, in a good way. He comes home on time. I never have to worry about where he is, or wonder about who he's with.

"I don't sit around wishing I were single again. Being single was never fun for me. Living alone was about trying to pay bills, chasing around after my kids, and dating guys I knew were too unstable or too uninteresting to be with for life. So I'm not wasting my time wishing I was single.

"Here it is, I guess—when you remarry you make kind of a tradeoff, really. You give up your dreams of that first marriage being perfect and lasting forever. You give up some of the dreams you always had when you were young—the way you thought your life was going to work out. Don't we all kind of have a picture of how our life will be when we're married?

"Remarriage is different than that. Maybe it's better, because you're more clear-minded and deliberate about things. Maybe it's not better, because we know that something before this has ended badly. Or maybe I'm just getting older, so I spend more time thinking about these things.

"What are you supposed to do? I don't want to be married to a cheater. When I'm around Kevin today I wonder how I was ever attracted to him. Kevin is just as young and stupid as he always was—except the years keep on passing by. Is Kevin going to be young and stupid when he's 60? Sometimes I wonder.

"Most times my kids don't want to have their visits with Kevin. They've gotten tired of his shallowness, and they can see through all his 'I love you' lines. If he loved them he wouldn't have run away with his girlfriend. Elizabeth, even as a teen, gets that in a big way. She loves Jim and calls him 'Daddy' at home. She tries to like Kevin, but she asks me why I ever married him. It's a good question."

■ ■ ■ ■

Ginny suddenly looks up at us.

"I'm sorry," she tells us. "I'm not sure what I'm trying to say to you right now. I don't want Kevin back, and I don't want to be single again. I certainly don't want a different husband than Jim. I love Jim—I truly, deeply love him, and I always will. I know he loves me, and I know he loves our kids."

Ginny is completely silent.

"And the rest of the story, at least for me, is this—life is never perfect, you know? I have a husband and a life that anybody else would admire and want, and why shouldn't they? I have it good, and I know I do.

"I'm not unhappy; I'm just aware of how my life could have worked out, and didn't. I look around and see so much brokenness, so much divorce, so much pain in relationships all around me. Even today I'm mad at Kevin for being such a jerk. Even today I guess I'm mad at myself...for not being able to see through Kevin before I married him.

"So what am I trying to tell you? I'm not sure. I don't regret marrying Jim. He's the best thing that's happened to me as an adult and as a woman. I am grateful to God for the life we share. My life is good and I know it's good—but I think people are supposed to keep their promises, and I think original marriages are supposed to last forever.

"That didn't happen for me. It's not happening for a lot of people.

"What I would say to a single mom, raising her kids, who is thinking about remarriage...is this. Go in with your eyes open. Don't expect getting remarried to solve all your problems or make your entire world better.

"If you're sad now, you'll probably still be sad after you remarry. You'll still have your memories and you'll still have to deal with your ex and maybe his family too. Being remarried won't change any of those hassles very much."

■■■■

After a long pause Ginny looks at us, noticeably brighter. "I would also tell her this: Choose your man a lot more wisely this time. If you've been married before, and your marriage has ended—learn from that. Don't pick another guy like the first one—a guy who is immature or abusive or absent all the time. Do yourself a favor and stay single until you find a man worth spending your whole life with."

Ginny stops again.

"It's strange. I sat down feeling incomplete, but the more I'm talking to you the more I realize how great I have it right now. I really did find a quality guy, you know? Maybe he found me. Or maybe God was at work. Whatever—the truth is, I'm in the kind of marriage where people respect each other and my children are loved and valued. The truth is, I have exactly the kind of remarriage I would tell single moms to try to find.

"This is exactly what I would want for my daughter, if she had been through the things I've had to go through. This is what I'd hope for Lizzy, if her first marriage were to work out like mine did.

"I guess I'm still sorting all this out," Ginny admits, "but really, my life is good. I'm glad I got a second chance. I truly believe this marriage is going to last for the rest of my life. That makes me happy for me, but even more happy for my kids. This time, they can see how things are supposed to be."

Ginny pauses, looking at us. We have nothing to add. Eventually she looks away and then back again, smiling.

"More than you asked for, right?" She laughs. "I think people want to hear that remarriage is breathtaking or fabulous or dreamy. And it is those things, but in a different way.

"When you get remarried—or at least when I did—your values change and you look for someone wiser, someone who is more of a grown-up. That means that maybe you're in a different kind of marriage than you had before—but that's a good thing, right? After all, look how the one before turned out."

Ginny looks at us, to see if we understand her.

"Does that make any sense?" she asks both of us.

It does.

■ ■ ■ ■

Where Would You Like to Go Today?

■ ■ ■ ■

There are many different ways to arrive at a place called single parenting.

In this book, we've talked a lot about single parenting after divorce. Much of our professional experience has involved families in transition: good people coping with difficult issues such as separation and divorce, raising children alone, getting remarried, and blending a family.

Yet there are other ways to become a single parent. Some never marry—the sexual and biological union that forms a child never becomes a loving partnership or a committed relationship. Although two persons were involved in making a baby, only one person stays around to change the diapers.

Others are single parents after the death of a spouse. As they work through the difficult issues of grieving and loss, they decide that staying single makes a lot of sense for their personal journey, and may even be the best choice for their kids. In spite of much well-meant advice to the contrary, they ignore the matchmakers and dedicate their lives to becoming a good mom or a loving dad.

These diverse pathways lead to the same place: single parenting.

Yet as we conclude these few pages, here's what we're really saying: Raising great kids is not about what you've done or where you've been. It's about where you're going.

Where would *you* like to go today?

■ ■ ■ ■

Regardless of the destination you may choose, here are some travel tips to help make your journey more meaningful and productive.

1. You Are Not a Defective or Inferior Person—You Are a Loving Parent

Some of us wear the social stigma of "single parent" as if it labeled us as abnormal, defective, or failing. But let's get real—you may be a single parent through no fault of your own. You're the one who's choosing to be responsible, to be the grown-up, to face life with maturity and wisdom. So how, exactly, does that make you "defective"? It doesn't.

Maybe you're a single parent because, when you were younger, you made some unwise choices. Maybe even some immoral choices. But that was then; this is now. Today you are a more mature, more responsible, more committed person. Defining your life by your past mistakes doesn't tell the whole story. And look closely at that little girl in your house—she's not a "mistake," she's your daughter. Nor is that little boy a "mistake"—he's your son. Your child is being raised by a loving parent, not by a defective failure.

Why do we allow the pain and guilt of our past mistakes to define how we see ourselves today? In the Christian faith, there is a concept called "new life in Christ," which is exactly that: *new life.* Writing to an emerging church in Corinth, Paul put it this way: "When anyone is joined to Christ, he is a new person; the old is gone, the new has come" (2 Corinthians 5:17).

As you learn to make wiser and more mature choices, celebrate the wisdom and the depth you are gaining as a person. Today is about new beginnings and becoming the best parent you can possibly be.

2. Your Children Are Not Orphans or Victims—They Are Blessed

When a deadly earthquake and the resulting tsunami destroyed much of Indonesia, it was a human tragedy on many levels. One of the worst aspects of the tragedy is that many children (who were younger, stronger, and healthier) survived the storms and lived through the floods while their parents perished.

There are many such children growing up in all parts of the world who do not have access to parents. For some, their parents are dead as a result of tragedy. Other children were abandoned by parents at birth. These children are being raised in state-run orphanages or in the overcrowded homes of distant relatives.

Still other children have parents—just not loving ones. These boys and girls are growing up in houses that are filled with anger, intimidation, and explosions of physical violence. The effects of alcohol or chemical addictions have destroyed the natural capacity of their parents to love them, care for them, and shape their world with respect and affection. These children have parents, yet their homes are places of suffering, not nurturing.

Your children are not among these unfortunate ones. Your kids have a mom or a dad who loves them, who wants the best for them, and who is working hard to provide for them. Your children are not victims: They are blessed.

Being single may be a fact of your life, but it is not a fact that dooms your children to suffering or loss. Having a loving mom or dad means that your kids are running the race of life with a giant head start over many other children.

3. Your Options May Seem Limited, but Your Choices Are Abundant

Did you notice how the single parents in the preceding pages set goals for themselves, kept on trying, and simply didn't take "no" for an answer? Whether it was walking around the neighborhood looking for a job (because they didn't have a car), or working at a coffee shop before finishing high school, these single moms and dads looked for opportunity in spite of their difficult circumstances—and sooner or later, they found good options.

Yes, it limits your choices to have a young child—or several young kids—at home to take care of. But no, it doesn't mean that you are stuck where you are, with no hope for a future. The real question is, where would *you* like to go today? It's time to start thinking and dreaming about that, and then taking small steps forward in the right direction.

Some people are naturally lucky. Most of us aren't—we have to work hard to get where we're going. We aren't born natural athletes so we have to practice. We aren't born knowing how to play a guitar, so we have to sign up for lessons. It takes hours of preparation and practice before most of us become truly "good" at something. Although we wish there were shortcuts, there aren't!

Instead of looking around at your limits, look ahead to where you'd like to be in a few years. Let yourself dream; and dream big. Then start making the small choices and taking the small steps that will keep you moving forward.

4. Build Your Team, and Your Team Will Help Build Your Family

The healthy, mature single parents we interviewed had another thing in common. They realized they didn't have to be "alone" to raise their kids. They reached out to parents, siblings, other relatives, friends at work, friends at church, nearby neighbors—finding support when they needed it most.

We have friends raising a child with serious and permanent impairments. They've developed "Team Casey" to surround this child with resources, care, love, and strategic ideas. Instead of coping alone with seemingly insurmountable problems and difficulties, these friends have built a support team—and now the support team is helping them cope and thrive. Good teams are like that.

Most days, you probably won't have people lined up at your doorstep, insisting that they want to babysit for your kids. Most days your mailbox won't be stuffed with cheery cards and gigantic checks made out to you. Instead, if you want and need some help, you will probably have to be the one to take the initiative, begin building your network, and start asking for assistance.

This is a very difficult step for some of us. We'd rather suffer alone than go through the humbling, awkward step of asking someone to help us. After all, what if they say "no" when we ask them? Here's what could happen: You could be in exactly the same situation that you're already in right now.

But here's what could happen when someone says "yes" to your request.

Your kids could gain a close and valuable relationship with an aunt, a grandfather, or a new friend. Your family could gain some much-needed help with car repair, home maintenance, or education. You could receive the help you need by simply looking around, finding people who are close to you, and asking them to get involved in the life of your family.

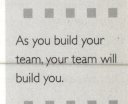

As you build your team, your team will build you.

Some of these people will turn you down for one reason or another. The good news is, a few will surprise you by helping even more than you dared to ask or dream!

In most cases it starts with you—you taking the initiative, you asking for help, you pointing out what your needs are. It is humbling and awkward, and can be unpleasant at first, but keep thinking about your kids instead of your own ego. What if you can get them the help they need, just by asking for it?

If you're involved in a caring church congregation, there are probably many people who would love to help you out but don't know what you need. Their hearts are in the right places, but their imagination is limited. Or perhaps they're too shy to offer help. Or perhaps they don't want to risk offending you.

It will bless those people to become involved in helping your family, so go ahead—open up and share your needs. Allow them the privilege of helping a family succeed and thrive, despite starting out with difficulty.

Even if it's only a few people, start building a network of helpers and caregivers who encourage and support you personally and who are helpful to your children. Be willing and available to help them, too—don't let the relationship be entirely one-sided. Be certain that you give also—and train your children to give.

As you build your team, your team will start to build you. Close friends and relatives will become much more "tuned in" to the needs of a family headed by a single parent. They'll learn how to give good gifts at the best time, and how to really help a working mom or dad manage the stress of parenting alone. Over time, your team will build you...and your children.

Grandparents, who may be retired after many years of working, often have the time and the energy to help. They just don't know where to begin! Your humble, direct requests can train them how, and when, to help. The same is true for coworkers, sisters-in-law, and others who already know you and care about you and your family. They're ready to help—will you let them?

5. Your Future Is Bright with Possibilities and Promise

Sometimes single parents get trapped under the baggage of the past: worrying about all they missed by having a child too early; worrying that they married the wrong person, which is why they ended up divorced. This fixation on past choices, past problems, and past issues spreads clouds across the horizon of their future.

Don't let this happen to you. Life's too short. Before you know it your kids will be adults and life will have rushed by while you weren't looking.

Get your head out of the swirling fog of past issues, set down the baggage you've been carrying with you, and decide to face forward. Instead of dwelling on everything you've done wrong in your life or every bad thing that has happened to you, start thinking about how to help your children experience the love and care of a healthy, mature, self-sacrificing parent.

Give your children a wonderful gift: the attention and love of a parent who is facing the future with optimism and hope, with confidence and good courage. Your kids can grow up knowing they are safe, they are loved, and their family is not merely normal—it's blessed in ways that many never achieve.

Can you face the truth? Then here it is: Your future is bright with promise and possibilities. The road ahead is determined by where you're going, not by where you've already been. So it's up to you. Where do *you* want to go today?

Resources for Single Parents

Divorce Recovery, Raising Children,
Remarriage Issues, and Other Topics

■ ■ ■ ■

Recommended Reading

Adkins, Kay. *I'm Not Your Kid: A Christian's Guide to a Healthy Stepfamily.* Grand Rapids, Michigan: Baker Books, 2004.

Broersma, Margaret. *Daily Reflections for Stepparents: Living and Loving in a New Family.* Grand Rapids, Michigan: Kregel Publications, 2003.

Burns, Bob, with Tom Whiteman. *The Fresh Start Divorce Recovery Workbook.* Nashville: Thomas Nelson, 1992.

Chapman, Gary. *Five Signs of a Functional Family.* Chicago: Northfield Publishing, 1997.

Covey, Stephen R., A. Roger Merrill, and Rebecca R. Merrill. *First Things First.* New York: Simon & Schuster, 1994.

Deal, Ron L. *The Smart Stepfamily: Seven Steps to a Healthy Home.* Minneapolis: Bethany House, 2002.

Frisbie, David and Lisa. *Happily Remarried.* Eugene, Oregon: Harvest House Publishers, 2005.

————. *Moving Forward After Divorce.* Eugene, Oregon: Harvest House Publishers, 2006.

Gillespie, Natalie Nichols. *The Stepfamily Survival Guide.* Grand Rapids, Michigan: Revell, 2004.

Hunt, Jeanne. *When You Are a Single Parent.* Cincinnati: St. Anthony Messenger Press, 2003.

Lauer, Robert, and Jeanette Lauer. *Becoming Family: How to Build a Stepfamily That Really Works.* Minneapolis: Augsburg, 1999.

Miller, Naomi. *Single Parents by Choice.* New York: Plenum Books, 1992.

Mulroy, Elizabeth A., ed. *Women As Single Parents.* Dover, Massachusetts: Auburn House, 1988.

Parrott, Les, and Leslie Parrott. *Saving Your Second Marriage Before It Starts.* Grand Rapids, Michigan: Zondervan, 2001.

Peck, M. Scott. *The Road Less Traveled.* New York: Simon & Schuster, 1978.

Smalley, Gary. *The DNA of Relationships.* Carol Stream, Illinois: Tyndale House, 2004.

Smedes, Lewis B. *Shame and Grace.* San Francisco: HarperCollins, 1993.

Smoke, Jim. *Growing Through Divorce.* Eugene, Oregon: Harvest House Publishers, 1995.

Tournier, Paul. *Guilt and Grace.* New York: Harper & Row, 1962.

Wagonseller, Bill R., with Lynne C. Ruegamer and Marie C. Harrington. *Coping in a Single Parent Home.* New York: Rosen, 1992.

Wallerstein, Judith S., with Julia M. Lewis and Sandra Blakeslee. *The Unexpected Legacy of Divorce: A 25-Year Landmark Study.* New York: Hyperion, 2000.

Wayman, Anne. *Successful Single Parenting.* Deephaven, Minnesota: Meadowbrook, 1987.

Family Centers, Organizations, and Resources

Association of Marriage and Family Ministries

Primarily a network of speakers, writers, and counselors working in issues related to marriage and family. Web site provides links to many helpful resources; this organization also sponsors an annual conference for workers in family ministry.

Web address: www.amfmonline.com

Center for Marriage and Family Studies

An educational center focused on helping families adjust to trauma and change, especially after divorce, separation, or abandonment. Four primary areas of study are: 1) divorce recovery; 2) single parenting; 3) remarriage; and 4) blended-family (stepfamily) topics, issues, and challenges. Speaking, teaching, and consulting.

Directors: Dr. David Frisbie and Lisa Frisbie.

Web address: www.MarriageStudies.com

Crown Financial Ministries

Teaching, training, and numerous resources in Christian financial principles, helping families and others manage financial resources according to biblical wisdom and prudent stewardship. *Among founders:* Larry Burkett (d. 2003).

Web address: www.crown.org

Family Life

Speaking, teaching, and special events for couples and families from a Christian perspective, including conferences and seminars. Schedule of upcoming programs and events listed on Web site. *Among principals:* Dennis Rainey.

Web address: www.familylife.com

Focus on the Family

A global ministry organization devoted to strengthening the family through broadcasting, publishing, speaking, and equipping. Produces and publishes numerous resources for many aspects of family life; some materials are available at no cost upon inquiry. Many other resources available for purchase or as gifts with donation to the ongoing ministry. *Founder:* Dr. James Dobson.

Web address: www.family.org

Getting Remarried

A wealth of helpful information related to the preparation and planning of a remarriage, as well as helping remarried couples with all aspects of family life.

Web address: www.gettingremarried.com

Instep Ministries

Programs, resources, and support for single, divorced, and remarried persons from a Christian perspective. Focus on reconciliation, restoration, healing, and hope.

Directors: Jeff and Judi Parziale.

Web address: www.instepministries.com

Institute for Family Research and Education

Resources and materials for families, including blended families and remarriages.

Directors: Dr. Donald Partridge and Jenetha Partridge.

Web address: www.ifre.org

Ronald Blue & Company

Christian financial management services, currently with over 5000 clients and managing over $4 billion US in assets. Focus on biblical principles and effective stewardship from a Christian perspective.
Founder: Ron Blue.

Web address: www.ronblue.com

Smalley Relationship Center

Teaching, speaking, and publishing resources for couples and families. Books, conferences, events at locations nationwide.
Founder: Dr. Gary Smalley.

Web address: www.dnaofrelationships.com

Stepfamily Association of America

Publishes *Your Stepfamily* magazine. Provides education and support for persons in stepfamilies and for professionals in family therapy. Numerous helpful resources and programs, many with local availability and access.

Web address: www.saafamilies.org

Successful Stepfamilies

Teaching, training, speaking, and publishing materials for stepfamilies, providing wisdom from a caring Christian perspective.

Conferences at various locations. Numerous helpful links to other related organizations on the Web site. *President:* Ron L. Deal.

Web address: www.SuccessfulStepfamilies.com

Counseling, Professional Referrals

National Association of Social Workers

The National Association of Social Workers maintains a network of social-service providers in each state, organized through its state chapters. By making contact with the chapter in your state, you can obtain information about providers of counseling and other social services in your city or region.

The NASW Web site maintains a database of information, services, resources, and members, which can guide you to locally available providers.

Web address: www.naswdc.org

■ ■ ■ ■

Information regarding the address and phone number of each state chapter is listed below in alphabetical order.

ALABAMA
2921 Marty Lane #G
Montgomery, AL 36116
(334) 288-2633

ALASKA
4220 Resurrection Drive
Anchorage, AK 99504
(907) 332-6279

ARIZONA
610 W. Broadway #116
Tempe, AZ 85282
(480) 968-4595

ARKANSAS
1123 S. University, Suite 1010
Little Rock, AR 72204
(501) 663-0658

CALIFORNIA
1016 23rd Street
Sacramento, CA 95816
(916) 442-4565

COLORADO
6000 E. Evans, Building 1, Suite 121
Denver, CO 80222
(303) 753-8890

CONNECTICUT
2139 Silas Deane Highway, Suite 205
Rocky Hill, CT 06067
(860) 257-8066

DELAWARE
3301 Green Street
Claymont, DE 19703
(302) 792-0356

FLORIDA
345 S. Magnolia Drive, Suite 14B
Tallahassee, FL 32301
(850) 224-2400

GEORGIA
3070 Presidential Drive, Suite 226
Atlanta, GA 30340
(770) 234-0567

HAWAII
680 Iwilei Road, Suite 665
Honolulu, HI 96817
(808) 521-1787

IDAHO
PO Box 7393
Boise, ID 83707
(208) 343-2752

ILLINOIS
180 N. Michigan Avenue, Suite 400
Chicago, IL 60601
(312) 236-8308

INDIANA
1100 W. 42nd Street, Suite 375
Indianapolis, IN 46208
(317) 923-9878

IOWA
4211 Grand Avenue, Level 3
Des Moines, IA 50312
(515) 277-1117

KANSAS
Jayhawk Towers
700 SW Jackson Street, Suite 801
Topeka, KS 66603-3740

KENTUCKY
310 St. Clair Street, Suite 104
Frankfort, KY 40601
(270) 223-0245

LOUISIANA
700 N. 10th Street, Suite 200
Baton Rouge, LA 70802
(225) 346-5035

MAINE
222 Water Street
Hallowell, ME 04347
(207) 622-7592

MARYLAND
5710 Executive Drive
Baltimore, MD 21228
(410) 788-1066

MASSACHUSETTS
14 Beacon Street, Suite 409
Boston, MA 02108-3741
(617) 227-9635

MICHIGAN
741 N. Cedar Street, Suite 100
Lansing, MI 48906
(517) 487-1548

MINNESOTA
1885 W. University Avenue, Suite 340
St. Paul, MN 55104
(651) 293-1935

MISSISSIPPI
PO Box 4228
Jackson, MS 39216
(601) 981-8359

MISSOURI
Parkade Center, Suite 138
601 Business Loop 70 West
Columbia, MO 65203
(573) 874-6140

MONTANA
25 S. Ewing, Suite 406
Helena, MT 59601
(406) 449-6208

NEBRASKA
PO Box 83732
Lincoln, NE 68501
(402) 477-7344

NEVADA
1515 E. Flamingo Road, Suite 158
Las Vegas, NV 89119
(702) 791-5872

NEW HAMPSHIRE
c/o New Hampshire Association
of the Blind
25 Walker Street
Concord, NH 03301

NEW JERSEY
2 Quarterbridge Plaza
Hamilton, NJ 08619
(609) 584-5686

NEW MEXICO
1503 University Boulevard NE
Albuquerque, NM 87102
(505) 247-2336

NEW YORK
New York City Chapter
50 Broadway, 10th Floor
New York, NY 10004
(212) 668-0050

New York State Chapter
188 Washington Avenue
Albany, NY 12210
(518) 463-4741

NORTH CAROLINA
PO Box 27582
Raleigh, NC 27611-7581
(919) 828-9650

NORTH DAKOTA
PO Box 1775
Bismarck, ND 58502-1775
(701) 223-4161

OHIO
118 E. Main Street, Suite 3 West
Columbus, OH 43215
(614) 461-4484

OKLAHOMA
116 East Sheridan, Suite 210
Oklahoma City, OK 73104-2419
(405) 239-7017

OREGON
7688 Southwest Capitol Highway
Portland, OR 97219
(503) 452-8420

PENNSYLVANIA
1337 N. Front Street
Harrisburg, PA 17102
(717) 758-3588

RHODE ISLAND
260 West Exchange Street
Providence, RI 02903
(401) 274-4940

SOUTH CAROLINA
PO Box 5008
Columbia, SC 29250
(803) 256-8406

SOUTH DAKOTA
1000 N. West Avenue #360
Spearfish, SD 57783
(605) 339-9104

TENNESSEE
1808 W. End Avenue
Nashville, TN 37203
(615) 321-5095

TEXAS
810 W. 11th Street
Austin, TX 78701
(512) 474-1454

UTAH
University of Utah GSSW, Room 229
359 S. 1500 East
Salt Lake City, UT 84112-0260
(800) 888-6279

VERMONT
PO Box 1348
Montpelier, VT 05601
(802) 223-1713

VIRGINIA
1506 Staples Mill Road
Richmond, VA 23230
(804) 204-1339

WASHINGTON
2366 Eastlake Avenue E., Room 203
Seattle, WA 98102
(206) 322-4344

WEST VIRGINIA
1608 Virginia Street E.
Charleston, WV 25311
(304) 345-6279

WISCONSIN
16 N. Carroll Street, Suite 220
Madison, WI 53703
(608) 257-6334

WYOMING
PO Box 701
Cheyenne, WY 82003
(307) 634-2118

Thanks to Our Partners in Writing

■ ■ ■ ■

Writing is a partnership among authors and many others. Although the names of the others do not appear on the covers or the bylines, these dedicated professionals are highly responsible for the final form and content of a book.

We are forever grateful to the committed team members with whom we partner at Harvest House Publishers of Eugene, Oregon. Our primary point of contact is Paul Gossard, a recent finalist among his peers for the annual awards given by the Advanced Writers and Speakers Association. There is a reason that Paul has been noticed and respected by other editors and publishers—he brings a passionate excellence to everything he does. His careful and attentive work improves ours. We are grateful that his skill refines our raw material.

Terry Glaspey at Harvest House remains a genuine friend and mentor in our process of writing for publication. Terry's gracious example as an avid reader, author, and speaker often reveals to us the contours of deep Christian maturity. We learn from him as we move forward—Terry's influence on our lives is direct and meaningful.

Carolyn McCready served an executive role, caring for many areas of administration within the framework of publishing. Her interest in our work has blessed and inspired us. Her encouragement is a primary reason we have continued to move forward with the written word. Carolyn combines a gentle mentoring spirit with an educated reader's eye for good writing.

■ ■ ■ ■

A second bond of partnership exists between authors and booksellers. During our nationwide book tour for *Happily Remarried* we met some of the wonderful people who make our books available to readers through their attractive, well-stocked stores.

Two among these deserve special mention.

Dave Garcia manages and operates a church-based bookstore in

Vista, California. North Coast Church in Vista provides 22 worship venues each weekend (as of this writing) and ministers to around 7000 people. Dave oversees an operation that has kiosks at various worship venues and a primary bookstore in the main offices of the church. His employees and volunteers are among the most gracious Christians we have ever met.

Dave welcomed us for a two-day book signing event that was characterized by warm Christian hospitality. He and his team did an excellent job of advance work via publicity, signage, and direct mailing. We sat outdoors in a courtyard on the church's large campus, meeting a steady stream of readers, divorced persons, and remarried couples. Throughout all of this, Dave led the event with warmth and genuine interest. By the time our two days of signing were winding down, we felt like we'd made a new friend for life.

Steve Treder manages the Northwestern Bookstore in the Har Mar Mall of Roseville, Minnesota. Northwestern is a large, well-established bookstore chain with many outlets in the Twin Cities and beyond. The Roseville store is one of the most beautiful Christian store venues we have ever seen, filled with art, music, coffee, video areas for the kids, and many shelves of outstanding Christian books.

We arrived at Steve's location for a Christmas-season book signing. Steve met us just inside the door with a warm and genuine greeting. During our two-hour appearance on a Saturday afternoon, Steve and his team of workers brought us coffee, cookies, more copies of our book, and anything else we could possibly need. Steve's store was filled with shoppers and we were busy signing our names for the full two-hour period.

When you travel across the country to appear and sign books, you quickly learn to value the benefits of well-organized administration. Steve's welcome and his arrangements were absolutely first-rate; we came away deeply impressed with Northwestern Bookstores as a company, with their Roseville store as a location, and with Steve Treder as a Christian gentleman and a new friend.

■ ■ ■ ■

Lastly we must mention one other partnership in writing this book.

Although we conducted interviews and did ongoing research for nearly three years, the final writing of this book took place on a quiet, well-shaded college campus in the upper Midwest. Our search for a serene place to write led us (or was guided by God) to a Benedictine college on a hill high above the shores of Lake Superior. As we drove onto the campus for the first time, everything in our hearts and minds sighed with a sense of "this is it"—the beauty and serenity of the campus is immediately evident to all who are privileged to arrive at the College of St. Scholastica.

We are indebted to the great team at Residential Life who found us a place to live and write for a few months. Jessica Johnston welcomed us and spent the next few months anticipating our every need, rushing to our aid with help and good humor at all times. Jessica excels at serving others and managing events. Samantha Bugni helped host hospitality times on campus and always displayed generous Christian warmth in all she did. Beverly Beaudette served as the leader and manager of the Residential Life team; her energy and enthusiasm for life are contagious and inspiring!

We were daily visitors to the well-stocked campus library, enjoying the knowledge and helpfulness of many on the library staff. Among these Karen Ostovich was a constant source of help and information. Somehow the staff seemed to never tire of us, even though we were invading their space frequently!

Another key aspect of campus life was the mailroom, through which passed all manner of communication between us and Harvest House. Whether sending or receiving items, the mailroom staff quickly learned our names and treated us like trusted friends. Overseeing the efficient administration of the mailroom was Keith Haugen; we also received constantly cheerful help from Phil Hohl and Kimberly May. Going forward, we'll miss seeing Phil and Kim every weekday!

In places where the prose of this book flows with open grace, you may be sure that the beautiful campus of St. Scholastica imparted its gifts to our writing. We strolled among the gardens outside the monastery, visited the chapel for vespers, walked the boardwalk along Lake Superior, and interacted with students, faculty, and staff of the college. In all these things we were greatly blessed by our sojourn among the Benedictines. We are forever grateful.

David and Lisa Frisbie
Psalm 63:1-2

About the Authors

For more than 25 years, Dr. David and Lisa Frisbie have been learning about family life. As directors of The Center for Marriage & Family Studies, their attention has focused on families in transition—helping families adjust to trauma and change.

The Center for Marriage & Family Studies pursues four primary aspects of learning and growth: divorce recovery, single parenting, postdivorce remarriage, and family life in blended families (stepfamilies). Offering seminars, retreats, workshops, and courses in these four areas, the Center provides effective resources so families in transition can become places of health and wholeness.

David has spoken at retreats, camps, and conferences since 1973. He and Lisa are the authors of several books and numerous articles on topics of marriage and family life, with special emphasis on families that are experiencing change.

Their ministry of encouragement and healing has taken them to each of the 50 states, 11 of Canada's provinces, and more than two dozen other nations of the world. They have greeted audiences small and large, from many cultures, with words of hope and healing, with good humor, and with topical, up-to-date scholarship.

Media appearances by the Frisbies include those made in *USA Today,* the *New York Times,* and numerous local journals. They have been interviewed on ABC-TV and CBS radio, as well as on many local broadcast stations.

David and Lisa have been married for 28 years and make their home in Southern California.

By design, The Center for Marriage & Family Studies is nonpolitical. It neither endorses candidates for elective office nor provides voter guides. It is not affiliated with any church, congregation, or denomination. Neither the Center nor its directors comment on pending legislation or other political issues.

Further information on the Center's programs and activities can be obtained at www.MarriageStudies.com.

- To schedule a presentation or program featuring David or Lisa Frisbie or both, contact:

    Lisa Douglas
    mountainmediagroup@yahoo.com

- To reach David and Lisa Frisbie, please use the following e-mail address:

    Director@MarriageStudies.com

- For information about the Center's resources and programs related to divorce, please contact:

    Divorce@MarriageStudies.com

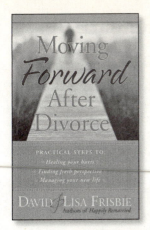

Moving Forward After Divorce

Practical Steps to Healing Your Hurts • Finding Fresh Perspective • Managing Your New Life

David and Lisa Frisbie

Is There Any Hope on Your Horizon?

More than 2 million Americans experience divorce each year...but you may feel like you're the only one going through it. After such a painful and even shattering experience, how can you start to move forward?

Authors David and Lisa Frisbie have spent more than 25 years learning from divorced persons. Here they offer the best strategies they've discovered—positive, encouraging ideas that will help you...

- raise healthy, mature children, even if you must do it yourself
- develop interests, dreams, and skills into new career opportunities
- find the friends you need to survive this difficult journey
- discover God's role in this new phase of your life
- understand your emotions and move toward healing and wholeness

Real conversations and real-life stories reveal clear, simple pictures of achievable steps—steps that will lead you toward new hope and new possibilities for your future.

~ Includes questions for growth and reflection ~

Read a sample chapter at www.harvesthousepublishers.com

Happily Remarried

Making Decisions Together • Blending Families Successfully • Building a Love That Will Last

David and Lisa Frisbie

What Can You Do to Beat the Odds?

In North America today, nearly 60 percent of remarriages end in divorce. In *Happily Remarried,* you'll find ways to build the long-term unity that will keep your relationship from becoming just another statistic.

From more than 20 years of speaking, teaching, and counseling, David and Lisa Frisbie understand the situations you face every day. Using many examples drawn from real-life remarriages, they speak with hope and humor about the challenges, leading you through...

- *four key strategies:* forgiving everyone, having a "forever" mindset, using conflict to get better acquainted, and forming a spiritual connection around God

- *practical marriage-saving advice* on where to live, discipline styles, kids and their feelings, "ex's," and finances

- *questions for discussion and thought* that will help you talk through and think over how the book's advice can apply to *your* circumstances

Combined with the indispensable ingredient of Scripture-based counsel, all of this makes for a great how-to recipe for a successful, happy remarriage!

Includes Helpful Discussion Guide

Read a sample chapter at www.harvesthousepublishers.com

Great Resources for Parents
from Harvest House Publishers

WHEN YOUR TEEN IS STRUGGLING

Real Hope and Practical Help for Parents Today

MARK GREGSTON

When you've tried everything you know to do, Mark Gregston offers this encouragement: Don't lose hope. From his 30-plus years of working with troubled teens, Mark shows you how to help kids work through their pain so they can enjoy the lives God created them to live. With this comprehensive guide, you can...

- develop a belief system your family can live by
- deal with the real issues causing your teens' troublesome behavior
- build healthy family relationships even in difficult times

WHEN GOOD KIDS MAKE BAD CHOICES

Help and Hope for Hurting Parents

ELYSE FITZPATRICK AND JAMES NEWHEISER WITH
DR. LAURA HENDRICKSON

Authors Jim Newheiser and Elyse Fitzpatrick speak from years of personal experience as both parents and biblical counselors, helping you deal with the emotional trauma that results when a child goes astray. They offer solid hope and encouragement along with positive steps you can take in even the most negative situations.

Helpful advice from Dr. Laura Hendrickson regarding drugs commonly prescribed to problem children—along with suggested questions you can ask pediatricians about behavioral medications—round out this compassionate, practical guide.

THE MOM I WANT TO BE

Rising Above Your Past to Give Your Kids a Great Future

T. SUZANNE ELLER

Your experience as a mother—and a woman—is influenced by the mothering you received as a child. Suzie Eller gently, compassionately gives you a healthy vision of the wonderful thing motherhood can be. From her own difficult experience, she shows you...

- how shattered legacies can be put back together
- ways to forgive, let go, and leave your parenting baggage in the past
- how to give your kids the gift of good memories and a great future